An Ode to Love and
Being Loved

An Ode to Love and Being Loved

An Anthology of Writings and Poems

By Judith Küsel

Professional typesetting by www.MYeBook.co.za

ISBN: 978-0-620-80515-5

Table of Contents

Introduction.. vii
Dedication xv

1. BACKGROUND 1
Chapter 1. An Ode to Love 3
Chapter 2. Karmic cords and Links –
Relationship patterns.. 11
Chapter 3. Karmic Links 19
Chapter 4. Soul Quest.. 41
Chapter 5. The Joy of True Union 49
Chapter 6. Love's many faces… 55
Chapter 7. Musings on Marriage, Twin flames,
Soul Mates 71

2. FEMININE DIVINE 85
Chapter 8. The Quantum Shift in Relationships....... 87
Chapter 9. The Celebration of Love......................... 95
Chapter 10. Letting Go 103
Chapter 11. The Bride is ready.................................109
Chapter 12. SHE...117

3. SACRED SEXUALITY 125
Chapter 13. How to harness the New Energies 127
Chapter 14. Male and Female roles in the
Consciousness Shift 133
Chapter 15. Sexual Energy 139
Chapter 16. The Highest Pathways of Love and
Being Loved 155

Chapter 17. Mystical Marriage –
the Ultimate Union.....................................161

4. WHAT ARE TWIN FLAMES? 169
Chapter 18. Twin Flame Love 171
Chapter 19. Soul Names, Groups, Mates and
Twin Flames 179
Chapter 20. The Cosmic Dance of the Twins 189
Chapter 21. The Illuminated Twin Flames..............199
Chapter 22. The Creation of Twin Flames..............209
Chapter 23. Twin Flames, Sacred Union and
Sexual Energies 217
Chapter 24. The Coming Together 223

5. LOVING...231
Chapter 25. Trust..233
Chapter 26. Touch 237
Chapter 27. I am Love 241
Chapter 28. The Music of the Heart 247

Anthology of Poems 253

Epilogue 277

References 281

Introduction

In *Twin Flame* Love, there is nothing as beautiful, as profound, and as sublime as when a man enters the sacredness of a woman, with all of his soul, a heart filled to overflowing with love, trust, presence, and fills her with all of him.

She opens herself completely and lets him into the sacredness of her inner sanctuaries, her preciousness, her whole heart and soul and all of her Being... The merging erupts into the sacred dance of the cosmic flames....

The sacred dance of the Ages.

In my sacred portal ....
You enter...
And your preciousness
Thrusts
Eternity's
Serpent
coils
Into
Infinity

Judith Küsel

I greet you with all my heart, soul and being! May

your hearts and souls also be open to receiving my message with great love.

We are standing on the threshold of an immense change in the way we live our lives – the New Age is not only dawning, but has already been birthed! It is no longer something in the far distance, it is here and now – with us in every single breathing moment, day and night. We are already living this transformation, whether we are conscious of it or not!

In the last few years I have been called upon to do *Twin Flame/Soul Readings*, and believe that this mission has to do with my own soul identity, and what I working with my *Twin Flame* essence, have retrieved from the *ancient memory banks*, including knowledge that had been lost to humanity. The significance of this will be fully revealed in the near future.

I have been shown repeatedly just how important the next ten years will be in the evolution of humanity. Nowhere will this be more apparent, than in the area of relationships. The old ways of relating are dissolving, and the patterns of behavior and lifestyle that have existed since the fall of Atlantis, are leaving us now!

It is no accident that so many of us have created negative patterns with our Twin Flames and in other relationships, which have come back to haunt us in this lifetime.

Not all relationships were forged in love – some were forged in times when dowry agreements were considered more important than anything else, and women became bargaining tools for political and other alliances. It goes without saying that many women were literally sold into slavery, into harems, and treated as mere chattels – to be used and discarded at will.

All of these patterns have been repeating themselves in our present day intimate relationships, in order to facilitate our inner healing. Women have to find love and forgiveness deep inside of themselves for the loss of their dignity, and their right to be the *goddesses* of their own bodies and lives. Men likewise have to walk the path of healing, for as the old control mechanisms fall away, some kind of balance must be reached, where the feminine and masculine forces can once again relate at a profound soul level. We will come to understand that when we love from our deepest hearts and souls, then the physical love has to manifest into form in the same way! For the soul is sacred in nature – innocent and pure. It can be no other in the eyes of the Divine, who created the soul in its perfection.

We have all experienced deep shame and guilt at some stage during our incarnations on Planet Earth. We have often felt ashamed at what happened to us, whether we were responsible for it or not. We tend to beat ourselves up, or feel that we should have had a better deal in life. Shame and guilt can be perpetuated over many lifetimes, as the old negative patterns, cords, attachments and hooks in our sexual areas, still keep us tied to those who entered them, even from lifetimes ago!

I believe that higher healing is now going to be-come the norm, as balance returns to humanity. For a time in Atlantis, insanity reigned, now sanity is returning, and so our deep soul wounds and scars will have to be opened to their very core, in order for us all to heal – both men and women.

We are all essentially one and the same, whether we abused our power, or were abused ..... The true and deep lesson for humanity lies in the correct use of both power and love.

We will now be forced to delve ever deeper into our relationships, not only with our *Twin Flames*, or other soulmates, but between ourselves and the Divine. It will mean shedding skin after skin after skin – until there is just the naked soul in all its glory and innocence, in its true relationship as Son or Daughter of God, and in the role of co-creator.

What is it that we wish to create with our relationships?

What do we wish to create with our love for each other?

How is our love relationship going to serve the rest of humanity and the Cosmos at large?

How are we both going to fulfill our highest soul purpose and calling, while still finding that deep love for our partner, and serving by loving each other in new and sacred ways?

How are we going to use the *sexual fire* for the greater good of all, in higher service?

In the *Ancient Mystery Schools* the soul endured stringent initiations into the rites of *Love and Sexual Energy*. Both were considered the most powerful gifts that the Creator God had bestowed upon Creation!! Read this again please: *the most powerful gifts bestowed*.

It is what we do with these supreme gifts that

makes or break us!

The Ancients knew this!

That is why one had to go through initiations, to develop inner strength and fortitude, so that the soul self could be trained to find that deep love within – a love that would sustain one, no matter what life brought, in the form of both challenges and support. Once the soul was deeply anchored in Divine Love, it was able to deeply love itself, and when it truly loved itself, it could then love the other in the same measure as the love for self, and the love for the Divine was present – The *Sacred Trinity*!

For in any relationship there are not only two souls involved – there is the *third force,* which is the governing energy, the *Divine Power* itself.

In true *Sacred Union*, there is a heartfelt honoring of the other, and a profound appreciation that the Divine lives within that soul, as it lives in the body, the mind, and spirit. There is also a deep respect for the power of sexual energy, for when it is used correctly, then egos have to get out of the way, and a *sacred flame* is ignited, which will singe, burn and harm if not understood fully.

It was no accident that those men who historically had powerful life missions to fulfill, always had a *Twin Flame* with whom to perform these ancient sexual rites, due to the fire of the *sacred flame*. The woman, more than the man, is the transmitter of this energy, and **he** can only step into the fullness of his own power and the maturity of his mission, when **she** is completely empowered within. I repeat – she has to be totally empowered at a deep soul level.

Therefore true maturity, true wisdom, and the exact initiations were only considered to have been fully attained and activated at the age of 60!

Then one was recognized as finally having come of age, able to understand the deeper *Mystery,* and to use its power responsibly. All the preceding years were spent in initiation, so as to step into full power at 60 years old. If was also by design that when these sexual rites were performed in maturity, that the next fire was ignited – the *fire of longevity!* One could literally extend the life span, by finally understanding the deeper mystery of *Twin Flame* union, and all the energies involved.

If there is divergence or inequality within the male and female relationship, then there is imbalance, creating immense pain and suffering in many forms!

This means that the man must stand in his full power, not with brute force, but tempered by deep and abiding love, with a full understanding of the *Mystery of Love and Life,* to which even he must bow, and be flexible within.

The woman also has to stand in her true strength – which is anchored in her womb, her sacred soul self, her emotional center. She has to be fully empowered by the *Mystery of the Spirit and Soul*, and all that is *Love* at its deepest depths. She can only transmit the *Sacred Fire* via her womb, if she is firmly anchored into the *Mystery of the Goddess* herself, for she *becomes the Goddess* in the sexual act! If she is not thus empowered, she will go off kilter, and will then withdraw from the male, because she is not in harmony with the supreme balance of Life itself.

See, then how much humanity has lost – how much we have to remember and re-learn!

Only when we truly seek with all our heart and soul to love another as we love ourselves, and love the Divine above all, can we experience the very depth of the Mystery of the *Sacred Fire* itself.

Such is *Cosmic Law!*

If one does not honor this *Cosmic Law*, one will reap what one has sown, causing pain, suffering, and destruction.

Essentially, achieving the higher state of *Balance*, lies in the deep understanding of soul relationships, and in a higher comprehension of the sexual energy, namely the *Sacred Fire*.

Without that we cannot truly find new and higher ways of loving each other, nor discover the beautiful *Sacred Union* which is the ultimate gift from God.

May the next years bring this understanding to all who are reading this now.

This is an adventure, and a deep unfolding in itself, and only those who really seek with an honest and open heart, will find the keys and codes given to them to unlock the *Sacred Fire*.

Such is the importance of this time!

May those who have ears to hear, truly hear!

Dedication

I have come many lifetimes with you on this planet, some good, some bad, and some just plain traumatic. I have been with you through parallel lives and other galaxies, star systems as indeed the cosmos is our playing field!

I have been through all the gamut of emotions with you, through all that life can bring in whatever form and since the beginning of when we were born as souls.

What I have found is that love has not dwindled through it all. How could it?

It changed form, yes, and sometimes I saw more of the shadow in you than the light, and vice versa. And sometimes we both pushed each other over the edge, but somehow found each other again and again.

So how can I not love you? I do.

And it matters not what other form or existences, or cosmic sojourns come, that love will abide through it all. So how do I love you?

If I could count the thousand ways my soul expresses itself through all existences, I would end up with the uncountable, and it is too much for my human mind to comprehend. So I will not try to analyze, nor question.

I just love you. Full stop, no? Not full stop – just ad infinitum. Perhaps love is best expresses itself when eye meets eye, soul meets soul.

The soul needs no words. It knows only infinite love and sees no end nor beginning nor all the illusions the worlds spin in and around us.

Loves infinite loving...... Loves. Ad infinitum....

I bow to the Power of Love and I ask for its anointing, so that I can open myself to love even more....

Judith Küsel

BACKGROUND

Chapter 1

An Ode to Love

Eye meets eye...
Soul recognizes soul...
And the eternal dance of Love is re-ignited
from eternity....

Slowly the realization is dawning, that meeting your *Twin Flame* might be like meeting the other half of yourself, while still bringing its own challenges.

I am writing this today because of letters I received where the writers have met their *Twin Flames* (or presume as much, for often soul mates are confused with *Twin Flames*, or the infatuation is such that one believes this person to be a twin, when it is not so). Perhaps the sex and communication is great, but the reality may be that the twin is not free or is cannot be fully present in the relationship, or is behaving in a manner which is causing the partner pain.

Sometimes patterns created over many lifetimes, come back to haunt us in this life, and unless they are released and new ones are created, the same old destructive patterns will repeat themselves. For we were not all angels in previous lives – indeed some were anything but! That is why I love doing soul readings, for it will pinpoint where the pattern started, and how it is being repeated in this lifetime.

Relationships on this planet cannot be based just on sex, however wonderful it is. In the beginning, there is unbridled ardor, and then later couples wonder how to reignite the spark as a different reality starts dawning. For after the infatuation wears off, you still have to endure the habits of your partner which can irritate the living daylights out of you, or the ex-spouses, children, and everyone else who was already there before you met. The former partners don't just disappear, nor the children, nor the parents, nor the friends and families. When chaos is created, it will remain chaotic until order and balance are restored.

Any relationship has great hidden lessons, and *Twin Flames* who mirror each other more than any other relationship, are faced with the biggest challenges. Yes, it is a trial to love yourself totally, utterly and completely, warts and all, shadow and light, without a mask to hide behind, and then also to love another.

For instance, the twin might be a part of your own soul, but the lighter you are, the darker they may be, the more of a perfectionist you are, the more laid-back they could be. You may be brilliant with money matters and a billionaire, but your twin may have no sense of money and spend everything etc.

In Afrikaans they have a lovely term to describe this: *"die klein jakkalsies"* (the little jackals). In the beginning you can be so sexually infatuated and addicted to each other like adrenalin junkies, that those little jackals are not noticed – like him squeezing the toothpaste in the middle, while you neatly roll it up! You could be happy-go-lucky and your partner could dissect and analyze everything. You may love others just as they are, and your twin may prefer to label everything, which could include labelling you and wanting to control you.

To me this is the trump card: **The Joker**.

The Joker is the "trickster" since *Twin Flames* are obsessed with each other. He appears to teach us a beautiful lesson: *You cannot make anyone else happy nor fulfil them.* It is impossible – even if it is your *Twin Flame*.

So you may be having this orgasmic sex, and then he/she just jumps out of bed, dresses to return home to their spouse (or to their laptop and work), after all they have commitments and obligations there, for as much as they love you, they love their job, their kids and current spouse too (even if they say they hate their significant other –they still care for them on some level). You think to yourself: "Have I not satisfied him/her? Have I been too much or too little?" And beat yourself up.

And the Joker sits there and has a good laugh......

The fact is no one else can make you happy, in the same way that the twin did not necessarily make their previous partner happy, they cannot grant you perpetual joy either, as no one is God.

Only you can make yourself happy, decide to do the inner work necessary to love yourself deeply, so that whether another is in your life – or not, it makes no difference. If they are there, ideally, you do not attach to them so much that you're miserable when they leave. For as much as you may adore having another there, to the same degree you must love being by yourself, and enjoy your own company. So if they were to suddenly disappear with another, then even if you are temporarily traumatized, you can carry on without them.

If you feel needy, and whine about how little you are loved, you will become even needier. Nobody enjoys being with such a person, and are more likely to leave such a relationship.

The more empowered you become from deep inside, the more you love yourself and nurture that depth of soul and joyful beingness inside you, the less needy you are. The more you enjoy your own company, and love conversing with your soul, nurturing yourself, body, mind, spirit and soul, the less you need someone else to make you happy.

That does not mean that you don't wish to be in a relationship. It is just that you are so content with yourself that you can love another freely without trying to own, manipulate, or control them, nor be constantly begging for love. There is something immensely attractive and sexy about someone empowered from deep within.

They emit a radiance, and an inner state of balance and equilibrium which shines through everything. They do not need to be perfect, or beautiful in a worldly sense, but when they enter a room, they have a noticeable presence. They have done their inner work and come to love themselves totally and unconditionally and then, when they meet up with someone (note: someone – not necessarily the twin) they can love wholeheartedly, without attachment. That means they love so much, that even if that special someone is taken away from them, their complete love will still be present, under all circumstances.

Why? Because they know that love is eternally there. Love has been there ad infinitum. It does not matter how the other is behaving, or not behaving, doing or not doing in this life – you love that soul – no matter what, just like you love yourself – unconditionally.

You love because that is the state that you are constantly in.

That state cannot be affected by anyone else – for you are solely in control of your inner equilibrium. That is your heart domain, and you can't always choose the circumstances, or events, but you can choose your reactions.

When you move back into your heart and soul, you will see the importance of doing the inner work, as it is clear that even if you switch partners like shoes, the emotional baggage remains, unless you release it. Many chose to carry baggage from one relationship into the next and the next and the next, repeating the same old patterns. Changing partners does not solve anything, indeed it gets worse, and may end with them blaming their partners for their own inner unhappiness, when in reality they have not healed themselves.

So, remember that with your *Twin Flame*, any short

comings will be amplified, because they will mirror back to you everything that you have not owned, or made peace with deep within.

No one can skip the inner work. You can try, but it will come in the form of *the Joker*, until you finally understand and master the lesson.

That is the reality of life.

Yes, your Twin Soul can and does bring ecstasy, bliss and euphoria, but they will also highlight the need for your own inner work to be done, so that you may make peace within your own heart and achieve total bliss and harmony.

I sought for space…

For distance…

I wanted more and more…

And in the process

Now unfolding…

I pushed you far away….

I searched and searched

For answers…

I travelled a thousand miles…

I looked for sages…

Ancient lore…

Then, suddenly – AHA!

The Light has struck…

I look…

I see..

I am COMPLETE!
Completed…
I am roaming free…

You are completed too
Yes… free!

I am the circle…
So are you….
Love comes from deep WITHIN…
It overflows two circles…
And in the quarter half…
Conception is achieved,
of overlapping love…
"T'is Love – OVERFLOWING…
AD INFINITUM…

I realize that Love…
Lives on….
Is there…
And Stretches out…
A flowing flow…
For AD INFINITUM…
YES, AD INFINITUM….

I stretch my arms…
Reach out…
As we embrace as ONE…
There never was a you

Nor me…
Just Love…
Meeting Love…
AD INFINITUM….

Free flying you…
Free flying me…
Love… AD INFINITUM….
Yes, AD INFINITUM….

Judith Küsel

Chapter 2

Karmic cords and Links – Relationship patterns

Through my *Twin Flame* soul readings, which mainly deal with relationships, and in my own life experience, I have encountered certain karmic patterns which have been created over many lifetimes on Earth.

In essence this is not about *Twin Flame* relationships per se, but rather about **patterns** created between two souls in the context of a relationship, whether married in a past life, as lovers, or in whatever form their connection was.

There are both positive and negative patterns. I was shown that when positive cords and patterns are created, they have a beautiful and profound spectrum of pure love and light. Within these sacred geometrical patterns, the **Flower of life**[1] appears as if lit up from deep within, like a star-filled galaxy, with all the color spectrums of light radiating from it. These are loving cords and ties which are formed in moments of pure and utter love. These are moments when the ego

---

[1] **The Flower of Life** is a name for a geometrical figure composed of seven or more evenly-spaced, overlapping circles. This figure, used as a decorative motif since ancient times, forms a flower-like pattern with the symmetrical structure of a hexagon. Wikipedia.

disappears and true oneness is experienced on multiple levels. Such patterns are always uplifting and eternally there, for they are created from the purity and essence of Love, in its most beautiful Divine form.

However, dark patterns and those infused with trauma, pain, betrayal, jealousy, lust, control and ownership are filled with shadowy strands. Some of these cords and ties are seen as slimy black entities; some appear as dark tentacles hooked into the body, linking two people together for lifetimes. Others have the appearance of a spider's web, filled with dark viscous matter. This is how I have seen and sensed them in myself and others.

These patterns between two souls reflect the collective consciousness of humanity, since the balance between masculine and feminine energies becomes distorted, and ownership of each other becomes the norm. Often marriage was a means of obtaining a dowry, so an individual was sold off to another party, because of political and property alliances and thus was not necessarily a union of love. Other individuals were enslaved and used as concubines, or eunuchs, or merely regarded as possessions, with neither feelings nor soul.

The problem with such relationships is that due to these karmic links and ties, these souls will be drawn together for previous marriage vows, sale contracts, or political alliances and are still in place in the ethers. So when soul meets soul, one partner may still feel they "own" the other, and therefore they may still demand this right of ownership in the current lifetime. Unless these old vows and contracts are released, the angels administering them keep them in place.

Often, due to such soul contracts, souls will be drawn into relationships, even those based on negative patterns, for they now have a window of opportunity to release these outdated vows and pacts and to dissolve the unhealthy patterns. Yet, some souls get so caught up in love and hate relationships that they just tend to repeat the same pattern.

This pattern is exacerbated when the man in question has had a harem during a previous lifetime. So now he may still have this impulse to want to possess more than one woman, and likewise this could manifest in a woman wanting to have more than one man. So, this idea that someone could "own" more than one partner could manifest, often with little or no understanding, especially if the chosen other is not party to this practice. Perhaps there could also be a past trail of intrigue and jealousy with these other partners, which can also make itself known in the present life in the form of unreasonable jealousy.

If you think of your soul as having had *multiple existences in various forms*, then you will realize you have also have had a myriad of relationships, and at some time this lifetime you could meet up with some of these souls. Then there is that instant attraction, and that sense of familiarity – because of past connections and events.

Any and all relationships have amazing lessons to impart, and maybe the greatest lesson of all is to *never give your power away to anyone or anything*.

To me one of the most incredible things happening

13

now is the return of the *Divine Feminine* to Earth, as souls incarnating as women now have the opportunity to step out of any slave mentality; either political or property pawn enslavement, to claim their birthright. So now we can cut those *negative cords* and attachments to free ourselves from old vows, contracts and enslavements to become liberated in all aspects.

As women reclaim their power, ideally they will grow in love. As they start their inner house cleaning, the collective consciousness rises, and the new woman emerges. She moves into the heart of compassion, forgiving the past and releasing pain and trauma, thus empowering herself on all fronts. The feminine power is different from the masculine, for it is heart-centered and compassionate at its core.

This does not mean that men were never enslaved or owned – of course they were, and many men are now embracing the feminine side of themselves, which is leading to a more balanced planet.

Your soul is an immortal Being and since the beginning of time when you were first created, you have a hidden history, a memory bank. This is the **Divine Blueprint** of your soul and it is who and what you truly are.

When you incarnated on this planet, you forgot this. There might have been moments, as a child when you remembered, but the adults never listened and tried to prevent you from talking. As time went on, you forgot those childhood memories.

We are now entering the time, when this blueprint will be fully activated once more. As the dimensional shift happens, and the frequencies and vibrations of this planet rise, the old memory banks will increasingly be triggered.

You might find that you have strange and vivid dreams, or spontaneous moments of complete recall. You might see yourself in different garments, with more or less the same face; you might appear as a man or woman, child or elder.

Some will find themselves inexplicably drawn to another part of the globe while others may be drawn to objects that just show up on their path, or be fascinated by things they never would have looked at before.

There is always a sense of familiarity, a deep inner knowing that you have been here before, have worked with this before, have studied this, taught this, dealt with the very same issues.

Total strangers who may appear as familiar to you become a long-lost friend or lover.

All of this is a mere awakening call, triggering your memory. Within this, the same old souls, with the same old issues will once again be brought together. These may have been issues that were not resolved in previous lives, whether on a one-to-one basis, in a group, or government.

The lessons which were not mastered or dealt with in all previous incarnations will come to the fore in the near future as events are escalating.

These issues were the same ones that confronted many of us in previous incarnations on Atlantis and Lemuria. This time round we have the opportunity to rectify these mistakes. We have been given the tools to do so, as this is the final opportunity to clear all past karma, once and for all!

I am merely emphasizing what is coming to the fore more and more, as the higher energies enter, bringing more cleansing and clearing. Nowhere is this more obvious than in the framework of relationships.

I see this as stepping into the powerful role of **Co-Creator**, where we now have the opportunity to dissolve old unhealthy patterns and to create positive and uplifting new ones which will be the foundation of the new way of life which is now emerging into the higher states of consciousness.

What a beautiful and profound gift this is! Wow!

In The Immortal Gardens of Delight

In the immortal gardens of delight

I wandered

As one in awe

Of wanton ecstasy....

Strangely in my inner soul,

I found that

somehow I could not find

that state

called

equilibrium...

For even in immortal halls

One sees

Reflected there

The strands of velvet dark

And hues of blues and browns…
With just a certain definite touch
Of orange and opaque's…..
With just the right sprinkling in
Of golden yellows
Golds
Indigos and pinks……
And whispers of all other shades
Of colours in between…..
For in the broader frame of life
All life is constantly in flux,
Transforming
And becoming
Something else….
It is the eternal Flow
Life itself then gives….
And what is new
Will once be old
And what is old
Is new……
Even gardens of delight
Taste sweeter
There by far,
When one has shed
A thousand tears
Of nuances of soul……
To dance the cosmic

Dance of life
To the infinite
Music of the cosmic spheres....
One has to twirl
And swirl and swirl
Embracing colour scales....
Vibrating
Frequencies......
And finding
That the ultimate delight
Rests in perfect.
EQUILIBRIUM
ATONENESS
Expanded Beingness.....
Contracting
In Itself......

Judith Küsel

Chapter 3

Karmic Links – releasing old vows, contracts, dowry agreements, and negative patterns

When humanity lost its innocence through the proverbial fall from grace, which was really a matter of free will and choice, and choosing the wrong option, this caused the separation of us from the Divine, the unified Cosmic Laws and the Tree of Life. As a result, karma was created and likewise the Karmic Board.[2]

Karma was basically created because humans willfully broke the Cosmic Laws, whether from free will, or at times out of sheer ignorance, so there needed to be lessons in balance.

All energy moves in a circular pattern, and at some point the *negativity created needs to be cleared and transmuted back into peaceful Love.*

We are given the lesson of experiencing the outcome of our actions or inactions, making wrong choices and ignoring the Divine and Divine Cosmic Laws of Creation, to learn the

---

[2] This Celestial Body is known as the Karmic Board, and its decisions are final in connection with the disposition of the affairs of mankind, except in rare instances where petitions are placed before the Sun of the System, and "Dispensations" are granted to accelerate the progress of the race. Chohan Morya.

correct use of power. Yet, simultaneously, at any given point of time, we also have the freedom to bring everything back into balance and to clear karmic debts, releasing any old harmful patterns that have been created.

It is therefore constructive to understand the fundamental Cosmic Laws of Creation, for all of Creation is perfectly structured, and rests on the foundation and principles of these laws. The laws serve as building blocks for the greater Cosmic order.

As original co-creators, we all knew this, and adhered to these laws, and therefore harmony reigned. We created from our heart space with great love, always aware of this greater Cosmic whole. We knew we were part and particle of this vast energy field, and that whatever we created, had to enhance and build upon and expand what already existed. In other words, the wheel had been invented, all we needed to do was to help perfect it – not to break it into a thousand pieces without the tools to reconstruct it!

I see this as very similar to a child who pulls a toy car to pieces, to see how it works inside and out, thinking he can create a better one, and then when only pieces remain, realizes he cannot put it back together again, and starts crying and asking the parent to restore it to its original form. When the parent can't do that, he throws a tantrum and pulls the next one to pieces!

That is basically what humanity has done time and again, creating the mess we all made, as civilization after civilization managed to destroy themselves. Our greatest collective lesson is to now let go of the past once and for all; to truly begin to master the cosmic lessons, and find our way back to wholeness again.

As with all things, wholeness, balance and healing all start with the individual soul. Every time, we enter into an agreement with another, it is recorded in our soul records. Every time we make a vow, or a commitment, it is recorded.

It doesn't matter whether these were dowry agreements, made by our parents in some lifetime, nevertheless a contract was signed. It does not matter how many business deals, political alliances, or whatever agreement we made in this lifetime or another, we signed a contract!

No matter how many marriages you have had in this or other lives, you signed contracts, and made vows somewhere along the line. Every time we repeat this and especially if this formed part of some religious ceremony, such as hand-fasting ceremonies, or blood vows, there are angels who administer them, and who will keep you to them – lifetime after lifetime, until the vow and accompanying angels are released and dismissed.

The same applies for poverty vows, vows of obedience, chastity, which religious orders often forced upon their members, and are still valid today, if not released! That is one of the reasons some people still believe in these outdated vows, apply them diligently, and then wonder why they never seem to make ends meet and want to give their wealth away! Unless these vows are released, the angels will keep you honoring them.

The Archangel in charge of all vows and contracts

is **Archangel Michael** and his legions of *First Ray Angels*. You can call for His help, and with the help of your own guardian angel, agree with their permission, to summon all those souls you ever made contracts or vows with, and tokens you had worn representing such vows (bracelets, rings, begging bowls, chastity belts, tattoos, etc.), to gather in a vast cathedral, along with any others who have ever witnessed you making such vows.

If you start doing this, you will be surprised at who you find there, and how many souls were involved – especially if you were a public figure in some past life. So be prepared to be amazed!

Then stand with *Archangel Michael* in front of an altar, with a huge Golden Book, the *Book of Life*.

He will summon one by one, all those who had any kind of vow with you, in all lifetimes, including all parallel lifetimes and existences, to ask if they are willing to release those vows, and are prepared to sign the Golden Book. He also asks all who witnessed the making of the vows at the time, to stand once again as witnesses.

When the Golden Book has been signed by the other contracted souls, he requests you remove any tokens you may still be wearing in your etheric soul form, e.g. rings, etc. which would bind you to the vow, and to place them into a bowl, one of his angels is holding, so that you may then be encompassed by the purity of the God energy. He then dismisses the angels who administered these vows. If you had tattoos or symbols ingrained into your auric energy fields, the angels will remove them.

Repeat this same procedure with **all** other vows, contracts and agreements.

After everyone has signed the Golden Book, *Archangel Michael* asks if you are now willing to sign to release all vows and souls forever. Do that! Then see how the whole congregation celebrates your release and your newfound freedom.

Once released, you will find that something deep within you starts shifting and being resolved.

You may have to repeat the process a few times initially, sometimes twice a week, and every week you may find new vows popping up, and something more needing to be released, as your soul memory banks are reactivated.

In this way we finally free ourselves and others from old contracts and agreements etc. which truly do not serve our highest soul good anymore.

As we move through our lives, we are continually drawn to each other, and read each other's soul frequency subconsciously. You will recognize a soul mate by subconsciously tuning into the frequency band of the soul group, as your own soul incorporates the same frequency band!

You might not do this consciously, but one thing will stand out clearly: It will feel as if you have known this person forever, and you have! One soul group consists of 144, 000 beings of the soul frequency band of your soul group, however, only a certain number will be on Planet Earth at any given time.

You may find that you do not even have to have

meet the person in the flesh, and can recognize them over the Internet, or even by just looking at a photograph (at least I do).

Mostly it will be as if you can relate to them on a deep level, with mind, body, spirit and soul. They might be in your family, or not at all. You may find that total strangers feel more like your real family, and seem to fit your soul better, than your physical family. This is why the eyes are actually the windows to the soul.

This is one reason why some people will never resonate with you, because they simply are from a different soul group, and thus vibrate at a different frequency. If you marry someone like that, you will find that at one stage or another you will no longer find a centre point, simply because you cannot, due to your different soul vibrations!

This is why, when you truly seek healing, your soul vibration and frequency, most often need fine-tuning to be brought into alignment with the soul group's frequency.

Never underestimate the power of your soul to remember!

My **Twin Flame Soul Readings** point to these contracts and binding vows, time and again, for most often we will be drawn to the same souls, and into the same relationships in this lifetime, because of these attachments still holding sway.

Life is a journey
Life is a journey

On which we embark
Little knowing
That
Although the map
Was given to our souls
Before we were born:
In the end, when all is said and done: –
It remains simply
A map!

We are born
And we cry
For now,
With our hearts still
Overflowing with the vision, the dream
The eternal flame of love
In our hearts –

We find soon enough
That the world has other ideas
And slowly but surely
The dreams and the visions
Are replaced
By the whims and wants
Of others
Who expect us to conform
To their own maps and
Visions

Of who and what we should be....

We are beaten and bullied
Into becoming
Something
That in our hearts
We know
We are not....

For the memory
Of Love everlasting
Of that map
the vision and the dreams
With which we were born
Stays buried deeply
So deeply
Within our psyche.....

On the outside
We pretend
That we are
What we are
When inside
We live
A different vision
And the dreams
Haunt us
At night.....

We walk our path
As best we can
But somehow
We get lost
In the jungle
Of cities and lifestyles
Foreign to that
planned
Into our maps.....

We lose our trail
As the jungle
overgrown
With nettles, with shrubs,
With ivy and thicket

We are so blinded
That we fall over
roots of the trees
And fall flat on our faces,
And lie there,
Winded,
Our faces and bodies
Covered with mud, ivy and moss,
Until we manage
To get up
And somehow
Continue along the trail....

Sometimes we meet those on the way
Who laugh at our plight –
"Can't you see that there is
An easier, better way?
Are you blind?

For there,
Down below is the huge highway –
Why, you can speed there – everyone
Does that, you know?"

So you follow them-
And for a while
You savour the speed
And you savour the endless
Rush for delight
That seems to consume
All those travellers
Who have not even the time
To look into each other's eyes!

For excitement looms
As more and more things
Need to be done
Or acquired: –
"The TIME is too short
To dawdle along
We want more!"

Yet, deep within the recesses of our souls
That map remains......

And one day
Weary and worldly-sick
We come to the time
When we are forced back
Onto the lonely trail,

And we find that somehow
We have lost our fear
For the jungle –
The trees, the ivy, the moss
The overgrown trail
Do not frighten us any more –

We find that we look at the trees differently
They become our trusted friends and
companions
We embrace the ivy and moss

And when we have time to look
Closely
We find the most beautiful lilies
And orchids hidden amongst
The overgrowth.

We find time
To smell their perfume

And marvel at their perfection….

At night we lie naked under the stars
And we look at the vastness,
The expanse of creation
And we feel small in comparison
With the infinite hand
That created it all….
The silent voice within
Speaks to our souls
And embracing it

Are embraced by such love and light
that we hear
that even though
All the stars are bright in the sky –
We are truly loved
And beloved
And held in the everlasting
Love and Light that created us all!

As the trail carries on
Uphill and downhill
Sometimes lingering leisurely
At other times
Climbing steep cliffs
With hands and feet
Closing our eyes

And trusting unseen hands
To guide and protect us
And carry us through

We one day realize
That we are content
Just as we are:
We have found the trail
Has led us to
Connect to something
So very deep inside of us
Which was and is always true to our soul
And our path...

We find that we enjoy our own company
We learn to embrace ourselves
And to love ourselves
Unconditionally...

We learn to dance the dance of life,
To play like a child again,
To frolic with the dolphins
And fishes in the ocean
And to laugh out loud
At the antics of some monkeys....

We fear not the leopard
Or the noises of the jungle animals at night –
We look into their eyes

And see ourselves reflected in there
And they sense our love
And send love back to us….

For the trail has led us
To conquer our own greatest demons
And fears ….

The silence has taught us to
Identify our own wounds
The soul wounds inflicted
By others
But mostly by ourselves:

As we were our own greatest judges
And our own greatest enemies
And created our own inner hell…..

We become lighter, much lighter,
Our souls start to shine,
We are illuminated
And we live each moment
As if it were our last –

We at last KNOW
That we are WHOLE
And that we are LOVED
By the everlasting LOVE ETERNAL
Which is unconditional….

We learn that we are worthy of love –
And worthy to love!

To embrace ourselves exactly as we are –
And love ourselves unconditionally too…..

So the path winds on
Until one day we find ourselves
Standing in a clearing
Overlooking the vastness of the turquoise-blue
ocean
And when we look up
We see snow-capped mountains
Rising high above us
Luring us onto ever greater heights
Of Knowingness ….

Our inner self prompts us
To continue our journey…

As we turn we suddenly realize that we
Are not alone
For there in front of us is a stranger
And we see at a glance
That this stranger
Has also fought his way
Through the dense forest
The soul path
For all the signs are there….

At first it seems strange
For we are not used to have someone
On the same path as we are....

We look into the other's eyes
And we find ourselves reflected in there
And suddenly we are lost
Between time and space
As we recognize
A fellow mystical traveller soul
As our twin flame
Part of our own
In fact the two halves
Of the one....

We find that words are not needed
What comes
Flows from the heart and the soul
And we sit silently
And we share the food
Of the mind, body, spirit and soul
We have gathered
From the abundance
That overflows from
The Vastness of ALL!

At first we feel the way around each other
For it is strange to suddenly have a companion

Where before
We used to travel and be on our own
And have learned to savour
Our own company....

Slowly but surely we start to share moments
Of laughter
Of reflection.....
sharing and comparing the stories
Of how we got onto the trail
And the adventures
That led to this moment
This spot....

And we recognize that this was no accident
That in that very map
That was written so long ago
This companion
And moment
Were already mapped out...

We first had to find
Ourselves
And know who we are
And to learn to accept
And love ourselves
Unconditionally
For who and what we truly are....

So did the other
And in that moment
You realize that
You have been given
A perfect travelling companion –

Someone to share your deepest
Visions and dreams
And know they will not laugh
Or ridicule
For they too have visions and dreams
That they want to share with you....

There are moments when you walk hand in
hand
Shoulder to shoulder
In perfect harmony
Yet there are moments
When you seem to have drifted away
As the other one seems lost
In a world of their own –

There are moments when it seems
That the other is pushing your buttons
And for one moment you forget
To love and accept yourself as you are –

Until you realize that this was but a moment
When the other was helping you

To identify, take out and heal the pain
That you have still deeply buried
In your soul

You need to cut it out
To bring it into the open
And balance it out
In order for it to heal....

You start appreciating the differences
As much as those moments
When you seem to be on the same wavelength
And all just simply flows....

Slowly but surely the love for yourself
Starts overflowing
And then a miracle happens
For now you realize
That the unconditional love and acceptance
That you have for yourself
Has extended to embrace the other
In unconditional love and acceptance,
too – And the other realized the same.

You are two wholes
Becoming as ONE
Within the embracing circle
Of ATONENESS
From which all love stems....

And in that moment
When the two opposites
Blend as ONE

The eternal dance of creation
Repeats itself

As the Divine polarities
Balance
And tremendous forces of Light
And Love are released

Which light up the whole of Creation

In one moment
You stand as co-creator
And you claim the inherent
Birthright of Greatness-
That you always had-
And which has always been
An inherent part of you!

So the eternal Cosmic dance of Love
Is re-created
And from this moment on
The map of your life
Flows into the other
And you start climbing
Those heights

One step at a time.....

Never in the other's shadow
But always in your own light –
It is the blending of both Lights
that changes
Not only this planet
But lights up
The whole of Creation.....

The eternal Cosmic dance
Is danced
To perfection
Once again....

And this repeats itself
For all eternity...

The moments embrace the WHOLE
And open arms
Welcome the ecstasy
And embrace
Unconditional love
That lives on
Eternally
ATONENESS
Bliss!

Miracles happen when love embraces love –

Unconditionally
And realizes
That this is perfection
The eternal Cosmic dance
Of Creation!

Out of one spark a WHOLE was created!
The journey continues,
One step at a time,
Until the life map
Has reached its ultimate end

And we return
To the ultimate
WHOLENESS
And ONENESS
Once again!

Judith Küsel

Chapter 4

Soul Quest

We are the sum total of many lifetimes and multiple existences in various dimensions and life on different evolutionary scales. Therefore we truly are not what we seem, just living here on Earth, for we can sink into a deep state of forgetfulness and often sleep our way through life and believe the programmed lies.

Nowhere is this truer than in the spheres of Love.

Deep down there is this yearning to find someone who will love us just the way we are. Fantasies develop, often around the concept of what life is reflecting back to us. It could be in the form of wanting a Knight in shining armor to sweep us off our feet. It could the eternal love stories of, for example, a Cleopatra and Antony. It could be the never ending search for the realms of the Gods and Goddesses of Love, whose eternal bliss becomes the essence of Nirvana itself.

What we are really searching for, is whatever completes us from deep within – to fill the longing, the void.

Essentially we are never told the truth, yet it will find us in the end. For the old equation, *as above – so below*, is one of the most vital keys to understand. The deeper we delve into our inner realms, and eternal infinity, which is our own soul, Soul Group and *The Infinite Soul*, the more we discover the endless possibilities of love deep inside.

Love moves on a high frequency, reflecting itself in the vortex energy, introduced by the Divine Feminine. It is the electro-magnetic current which is the life-force itself. It is no accident that the highest frequency energy places in the world and the pyramids, all work with this energy, for in principle it has the very same essence.

The Ancients left clues all around us, and they are incorporated into the *Flower of Life*, in the Cadeus, and in the symbol for the Tree of Life'.[3]

All these clues lead us towards discovering the essence, the Grail, the Holy and Sacred life-force. Yet, in order to find this Grail, we must first embark on a journey of discovery, which is at its core, a search for meaning.

Love and meaning go hand in hand, and therefore the love energy sustains us and keeps the flame of hope alive, and most importantly, in our darkest nights of the soul, it is this love that leads us home.

In his book *"The Search for Meaning"* Dr. Victor Frankl tells of his experiences in a Nazi concentration camp, where they were stripped and all belongings removed. He asks what made it possible for human

---

[3] **Tree of Life** The concept of a **tree of life** is a widespread my theme or archetype in the world's mythologies, related to the concept of *sacred tree* more generally, and hence in religious and philosophical tradition. Wikipedia.

beings to survive such extremes as the threat of gas chambers, and being stripped naked to their very core, of all vestiges of humanity.

He found the survivors had a cause, a higher purpose, a greater reason to live, so they had a vision or quest larger than just themselves, to focus on.

I remember reading this and wondering what gives my life this meaning, this vision, this question, that is greater than the sum total of just myself?

For the true higher meaning, the true love, the true inner quest, starts from deep within. It cannot begin from the outside for others will always have their own agendas and their ideas about whom and what you should be.

Sometimes when we love someone (and women especially tend to do this), we relinquish parts of ourselves, in order to please our lover. I have heard so many stories of those who gave up close friendships, in order to immerse themselves in the life of another. One day, if this partner walks out of their lives, or dies, they have no life support left, meaning that their circle of close friends and confidants has disappeared, and with it the ability to live independently.

(This by no means implies one should not enjoy close bonds with others. Rather we should never pursue love to the exclusion of other human relationships, nor the inner search for meaning. If you start living life solely to please your significant other, you could lose yourself in the process).

Essentially love, and all of life exists in a vast energy field. It starts within our own hearts and bodies, our souls, our emotional, mental and spiritual bodies, but most of all; it begins with a connection to that Source Energy, greater than ourselves, found deep within.

The *Tree of Life*, the source of all knowledge and wisdom, and the Quest for the *Grail*, all live there, deep within. The vortex energy, and its central keys and codes all lie encoded within us too. That is how we were created – for in essence we carry the *Seed of Life*, like the *Tree of life*, as a deep impulse to make someone else happy, or to wish for their fulfilment and happiness. When we finally find that *someone*, but after a certain time, no longer see them through rose-tinted glasses, we can feel let down, as our bubble bursts somewhere along the line. It is the same with material things – when we finally live in our dream house, we may find that void deep inside of us remains unfilled, so we search for the next "thing" and the next to make us happy.

The inner search starts with a very simple question: *"Why? Why am I here, at this time on this planet? What has my soul come in to do, be, and become? What is my unique contribution to life on earth? What gives meaning and purpose to my life?"*

Your soul quest, and calling, will always be greater than the sum total of yourself. It is like that invisible force that keep your fires burning, when it feels as if everything else is trying to extinguish them.

It is like a frail mother, suddenly finding the strength to lift a car off her child – in that moment her child's life becomes more important than anything else, and so she taps into a power deep inside, which is greater than her own limited beliefs about herself and her strength.

When you have this inner quest, all else falls by the wayside: relationships, jobs, everything. You simply know this is it!

The Knight searches for the *Grail,* leaving everything behind, as he journeys into the unknown, unchartered territory, with all the adventures which will test his inner strength and resilience, often bringing severe initiations and trials. Yet his Quest, his search for meaning, will help him endure and persist, until he finds his Grail, and ultimately becomes it.

There lies the crux. The journey is simply that which brings us to the discovery of the inner vortex energy, that higher state of being, of existence, of flowing, and then we become at one with it. This is what lifts us into the higher states of consciousness, into the state where we are able to experience miracles, and can operate on a multidimensional level. This is where the mundane become the magical, the enchanting and the extra-ordinary!

The Sorcerer's apprenticeship, was in essence the apprenticeship of the quest for the Grail, the alchemy of the *Tree of Life* itself, the *Flower of Life. Once it is found, one should* then "become" it.

There lie the keys and codes.

It is only in us becoming the quest that the quest becomes us, and we become that which we were searching for all along! Because when we live the higher meaning and purpose, we become that which gives meaning and purpose to all other life and life forms.

This is the central key.

Love me....

We stood in Immortal Halls
Before the Sacred Council of 24...
Our souls pledged to re-unite
When on this planet
Incarnate....
The Keepers of the Keys!
In all we had a MISSION,
A Pledge to come here and fulfil.....
A Mission GREATER than ourselves....

Our souls had known this

As of yore.....
So love me...
Simply for myself...
For sometimes being otherworldly...
For savoring moments
In the Halls of Immortality....
I find it hard sometimes
To walk with feet
Firmly planted on the ground....
Sometimes my vision
Expands where mere mortals
Have never trod before....

Yet, in the greater Scheme of things,
All is as should be....
For in the end,
What are we?
Mere Players in Immortal Scripts,
Acting out the parts
Assigned to us.....
To serve....
Yet, in the Serving
Are the Unlocking Keys: –
Here lies True POWER!
Rise with the Immortal Ones....
And Claim your potent Keys....
It is Love
And Love
Only....
This unlocks
The Secret Chambers....
And nothing ELSE!
LOVE IS THE IMMORTAL KEY!

Judith Küsel

Chapter 5

The Joy of True Union

At this time we are being challenged to simply find the mid-way point – the point of equilibrium in **all and everything** within and around us.

As the giant scales of life and love are tipping back and forth, it can feel as if there is simply no middle ground, as if all is in constant flux and flow.

We are being encouraged to find this balance, first within ourselves, within our own lives and the manner in which we choose to experience life from deep within our hearts, and then going outward to find this unity in relationships – whether romantic, or platonic, with friends, family and acquaintances.

Note here that I did not use the words: **mind, brain**, or anything physically based. The only term I used was heart, yet, this does not refer to the human heart, as you may imagine, but the spiritual heart, the soul heart, the feeling center of everything.

Over the past thousand years, we have slowly strayed from a heart-centered, balanced way of life, to being ruled by the *mind* with a more *masculine* way of thinking, relating and being. This has resulted in endless wars, which were no accident, for with the mind, comes ego-based living, where everything is focused on Me and **Us** and what we can get out of things!

The shifting of consciousness started in the 1960's with the *Hippie Movement*, as people began to question this *modus operandi*. They began to understand that something needed changing, and gradually the insight dawned that living had to become more heart-cantered. (That still entailed a search however, and some experienced the opening up of their third eye chakras, through using drugs, which did not necessarily open their hearts!).

Gradually conscious people began expanding their ideas, and the children born since early the 1950's, were those souls who volunteered to anchor in heart-centered living. They started to create an inward revolution, which helped bring about a change of consciousness, from a focus on the rational mind to a more heart-centered perspective.

On the threshold of any drastic change, all the ancient, outdated thinking struggles to stay alive, resisting change, especially any impulses towards inner shifts, for the old ideologies cling to the more familiar patterns of destructive living and relating. Previous patterns of a fear-based-existence, which have been repeatedly ingrained in the human psyche, and behavior, are held onto tightly.

When there is fear about expressing feelings, or relating closely with another person, or of simply living life consciously and to the full, then the old ways aren't threatened. Another issue has been control, as those who were able to control the minds and finances of the masses, could absolutely control the world.

All of this is slipping away, as the new is being born, and as we move into the Higher States of Consciousness, where the size of your bank balance is less important than your vast soul with its Divine connections.

I was shown a vivid picture of what is happening with the Earth's *kundalini* or serpent energies that are now being released, and gradually building up in potency.

This is affecting the way we relate to each other, and the very core of our sexual energy centres. If our relationships are falling apart, we have to learn to completely open ourselves up, and to stand naked in the light of *all that ever has been and will be.*

It is the open heart that opens up the keys and codes to our spiritual and sexual energy centres, and this has to do with purity of intent.

If your head is saying one thing, and your heart another, then you are out of sync with your own inner core self.

This means staying in a relationship even if we know deep down know it has spun out of control, and we are just not relating at heart level anymore. Your heart knows, even if your head is desperately clinging to the status quo!

So, what will happen? One day things will just go boom! Then all the glue in the world will not be able to stick it together again, unless there is a very deep heart-core change and the spiritual mind, heart and the sexual energies are tuned in and singing one song again!

This rising of the sexual energies, means that those whose hearts are wide open, standing in their truth and authenticity, will start experiencing magic in their unions, like never before. I am finding that these powerful energies are affecting us in such a way, that we are stepping into the power of being able to harness this energy in the correct way, and so can rise in dimensions, or octaves of higher consciousness. If we learn to do this from the heart and soul, with pure intent, it becomes clear that this energy force, can be used in Higher Service; with the understanding that the union is sacrosanct when I honour the Divine and sacred being of my partner, and he/she honours that in me. This makes for a transcendental union which is blessed in so many ways.

Beloved 2

Love letters from my heart and soul
flow etched with indigo sky
with the spurring fluffy whiteness of surf
to you…
As the most exquisite pearls
I gathered from the ocean depths of me…
waft forth with equal Love.
I gather
the thousand petals of my
heart-rose

closer

and

prepare

my inner-most sanctuaries...

with loving precious care..

And the spiral dances

into

Eternity...

Judith Küsel

Chapter 6

Love's many faces…

Odes to Love and the manifold faces of love, have been perhaps the most talked and written about subjects in life here on Earth over the last few thousand years. In fact, maybe for as long as we have existed, **love** has been the main subject of songs, poetry and stories. There is not a single culture in the world that does not have *Odes to Love* in some form or other.

Yet, throughout history, love in all its myriad expressions and forms, has often been misunderstood and misinterpreted, leaving us feeling as if we have missed out on something big in our lives, if perhaps we have never experienced the *Great Love Story* – comparing ourselves to *Romeo and Juliet, Tristan and Isolde, Antony and Cleopatra*, etc.

Have you ever sat down and really thought about it? All these great epic love stories had a sad ending. Juliet committed suicide, Tristan and Isolde were parted, and Cleopatra's life was a living tragedy. The list goes on: Helen of Troy, Isis separated from Osiris etc….

Yet, we still long for that ultimate love which will

be profoundly life changing. Most of us loved fairy tales when we were young, which usually ended in: "…..
And they lived happily ever after……"

Only in real life, that "happily ever after…." often finishes with the honeymoon (if not before) and can result in bitterness, regret, and sometimes downright ugliness, pain and misgivings.

Nevertheless, this has never stopped humanity from dreaming. In Languedoc, in the late 1100's and early 1200's the Troubadours[4] promoted *Courtly Love* and the *Courts of Love* existed. Love was glorified and troubadours sang songs about the Lady of the Manor, making her an object of adoration and love. Yet, that often meant that she had many lovers, and that the troubadour was perhaps her paramour himself, singing of her prowess in bed! What did this have to do with true love?

Why is it then that love, in its ultimate form, eludes so many?

Love and loving

In all of life there is *beingness,* a state of simply allowing the flow of Life and Love to flow unhindered, and then to become a transmitter channel for Love, which is the highest form of service that any soul can attain.

There are many forms of love and higher service,

---

[4] **Troubadours** – In the Middle Ages, were the shining knights of poetry (in fact, some were ranked as high as knights in the feudal class structure). Troubadours made chivalry a high art, writing poems and singing about chivalrous love, creating the mystique of refined damsels, and glorifying the gallant knight on his charger. Merriam Webster Dictionary.

yet when there is a *collective* to heal, like on Earth at this present time, then love is the only way to bring healing – there is no other.

However most have forgotten this truth, and the power of true love and the higher states of loving. So many lies are upheld as truth, and the truth itself has been distorted with hype and misinformation.

The higher states of love and loving are not found outside of the mind, body, spirit and soul, but inside. It is that profound inner connection the soul has to its collective over-soul or *Soul group;* to the Divine Source and to all of Creation, which includes a deep respect, love and reverence for everything created. For love is reflected, in a multitude of forms, in all that has ever been created and will be created forever more.

When we first began to separate ourselves from the *Higher Paths of Service,* we disconnected from this higher truth. Some started to believe that there was no higher path, and some believed that they were separate and not part of a greater connection to Source.

Some experienced an immense void, feeling neither complete nor whole. There has been a long history of soul decisions which reinforced this separateness, which I will not address now, but ultimately it created a feeling of not being enough or complete in ourselves, and needing another soul to feel complete.

In the process, much hurt, many emotional scars and immense trauma have been caused collectively, over a period of millions of years, as we completely lost the plot, and destroyed our knowledge of the holiness of all forms of life. In the process we also obscured the sacredness and sanctity of our own souls, and over-souls; the *Divine Source* itself, and thus all of Creation.

At this time, individual souls will be challenged to the very core to first of all find healing within, and to develop a deep, profound and unconditional love for themselves once again. Then, with this reconnection to our heart and soul, there will also be a reconnection to the Creator, and so to all of life.

When there is immense love for oneself, expanded 144, 000 times through the over-soul, and its' higher ranking Master souls, and then expanded beyond that to the Divine, this love is greatly amplified.

Love cannot do anything else than love! In its highest and purest form love cannot exist without extending itself, expanding upon itself, and so becoming a tremendous and powerful source of life itself, as the creator of life.

Love creates more love.

This is the highly sacred law of life.

Those souls who remember this path will always find ways to purify themselves from all illusions, fears, and "dis-ease" in any lifetime, even on a hostile planet such as Earth, as love can only be true to itself.

In the higher sense all souls are pure with the ability to be pure; in the same way all souls have love and are love.

The Creator of Love cannot create what is not love. Such is Cosmic law.

However, each individual soul has the freedom to choose for itself a framework to learn all the myriad expressions of life, life-forms and love. *There is a Soul blueprint, which has its unique pattern or form, its own soul name and its own vibrational frequency or tonal chord. It also, within itself will have the same vibrational frequency and patterns of its over soul or soul group and the soul group's collective expression of whatever trait of the Divine it has to experience and reflect back to the Divine source. It will also carry the innate vibrational frequency of the galaxy and the planet within that galaxy, for this is where it first was created to function or exist.*

Now, in the beginning love reigned on Earth, and the people had not yet fallen into forgetfulness. At birth, soul readings were done by the High Priestess in charge of the *Temple of the White Flame.* Then the Priestesses of the *Temple of Birth and Higher Teaching,* would program a birth crystal for the child; add a crystal of the Galaxy and planet of origin, and also add a crystal for the over-soul. Thus the child would be able, by holding the crystal in their hands, or wearing it, or placing it over the third eye, to tap into their collective soul all the time, and into the galaxy of origin, with its soul purpose or contract. This acted as guidance for the rest of his or her life.

The soul first of all has to connect back to its own truth, in order to reconnect with its purest essence of form, with the state of unconditional love and acceptance of itself. For essentially the soul on this planet seeks to reconnect to its *Higher Soul Self* and then to the *Collective Over-Soul* or Soul Group, which then amplifies its own abilities, and acts as a support group. So the soul is always surrounded, not only by angels and Archangels, who are there to assist and help, but also by Higher *Ranking Masters* within its soul group, the Archangels assigned to this soul group and to the Divine Source.

When that state of release has been reached, the soul feels the connection to the Divine more profoundly, for in being in tune with its own soul and over-soul, it then is in total union with the Divine as it was created to be!

This is the state where the soul truly becomes empowered, where love, in its highest form can flow freely and unencumbered, becoming what is deep within, and filling every fibre of one's being. We cannot be other than who we truly are – all else is an illusion.

When overflowing love is there, with the *Higher Soul Self* activated and fully functioning – only then can we truly step into the realms of a sacred and sanctified union.

For then we will merge with the higher soul self of our *Twin Flame*, or someone from our own soul group, and be able to merge to transcendental union.

For if one is too much and the other too little, one will burn the other and create more imbalance. Yet, if the two are equally lit, then this flame expands upon itself, lifting both souls into a far higher state of union, where there is enormous love for the other in every single cell and DNA structure of the body, expanding into the spirit, mind and soul, and then even further into the over-soul and the Divine.

This creates huge power and transcendent love, which is the ultimate of all loving unions, but can only be reached by pure intention, in absolute love. It is in fully accepting and loving the immense love vibrating in every cell of the physical, spiritual, mental and emotional bodies, as well as the soul, which all vibrate at this higher love frequency, that the union with another, activated in the same way becomes amazing! Then an extremely powerful creative force emanates from this Divine union, pure love in its highest form which extends to the rest of Creation like a ripple effect.

Many have forgotten this, but some are now re-membering!

There is serenity in a life lived in gratitude, in joy; delighting in everything. What's more, a shining, luminous, effervescent glow is generated, which seems to enfold the person like a shimmering cloak. A mysterious "something" that makes that person stand out in a crowd; – others are drawn to them, without truly understanding why.

True beauty of the heart is like eternity gazing back at itself in a mirror. Yet beauty is eternity and radiates forth, stemming from the very fires of a beautiful heart, shining outwards to touch lives everywhere.

For there are those, who are truly beautiful in soul, heart and mind, who sometimes feel so very forlorn and lost on Planet Earth.

They are the Earth Angels, incarnating here in disguise. They are beautiful souls, who shimmer and shine enchantingly, with eyes reflecting the exquisite loveliness of their souls. Yet, they are extremely sensitive; especially to anger, hatred, barbed insults, and the stinging arrows of cynical people.

They fall ill when surrounded by too much negativity. They run away from crowded shopping malls, for example, as they hone into the vibrations of the people around them, and have to shield themselves constantly from soaking up those negative vibes – they are natural healers, and the "St. Francis's" of this world.

They are the children, who will suddenly start crying in crowded areas, for they read others, and instantly shrink from the negative thoughts that some people send out.

They sometimes have great difficulty in expressing what they feel so deeply inside. Through all the hurts and pain inflicted by others, who may shun, hurt or ridicule them, they have learnt the hard way that the world does not appreciate their sensitive, beautiful souls.

They feel somehow alienated and different from others, and this can cause great bewilderment and pain, until they have learnt to love and accept themselves unconditionally. Then their eyes can open to why they are here, and the roles they have come to fulfil. Once they connect with like-minded souls, they blossom into a state of "beingness", which goes beyond the normal.

These are the Light workers who have come here to teach about love.

They are compassionate and empathic, and when they are serene, centred, and able to express their naturally loving hearts, they become role models of Divine love and peace.

Serenity is their trademark, and when everything is

collapsing around them, they are havens of quiet steadfastness and compassion, as the Divine expressions of Love that they are.

They tread softly on Earth, and in the lives of others, and are gentle creatures who just wish to love, love and love even more!

Anyone who finds him/herself deeply loved by these luminous souls, find that through the intensity of this love, they almost seem to be dissolved into a vibrational "beingness" they did not even know existed. These souls need to be treasured, and when they are, their partner finds a rare and precious jewel to be kept close to their hearts, who will embed themselves in their soul, mind and body. It becomes the true blossoming of heart-centred tender loving, beyond those of mere mortals.

Wherever they go, there are roses and lilies strewn in their wake! Indeed, they love roses and lilies, for both reflect the same purity and innocence which, when expanded becomes the true love that transcends all.

Love is a many-petalled rose, so treasure and nurture this exquisite beauty…. and your life will be immensely blessed.

When we are truly anchored in our heart chakras and have our higher chakras all opened up; we start radiating our light in extremely high frequencies. We resemble a Lighthouse, and become *beacons, drawing others to us,* mostly unconsciously, for they are drawn to our Light frequencies, vibrating and radiating forth.

As we grow in Light and Love frequencies, we start

to become *crystalline* – like a huge living sheer and transparent quartz crystal, pulsating with enormous electro-magnetic energy as *we shine! We are lit up from within, radiating out*!

In our crystalline form we can transcend time and space, we can become whatever we would like to become, travel wherever we want, as we are free to fly and to roam anywhere, for we are not encumbered by physical form any more. We are *transcendent beings*!

We still have all the sensations and feelings of physical form, but we are more than that, for we are now truly *soul-connected*, and not hemmed in by the control mechanisms of the mind!

We are so **at one** with all things that we *are* everything that was ever created, and everything that was ever created is us!

It is then that we truly understand that we are **Soul.**

We realize everything on the face of this planet is constantly being transformed, because Earth is alive with its own soul and so we start honouring, nurturing and loving that soul aspect.

We begin to act as co-creators, but now in a responsible manner, for we realize, that if we are everything and everything is us, all that we do or create, affects us as part of the whole! When we create we do so in love and harmony, for we are in sync with the whole.

The more we shine, the more connected we become with the true essence, the mystery that is life and love. We delve into the depths of whom and what we truly are, into the unfathomable realms of the great *Cosmic Soul.* We stand in wonder and awe. We grow in grace and gratitude. The deeper we go, the humbler we become, we lost our negative egos a long time ago. We simply grow, become...grow...become, more and more.

Love and light are soul companions.

I embrace the true companions of my soul!

One of the main reasons we chose to incarnate here, is to experience what life is like in such a dense physical place. Yet, some souls have added karmic links, through *the way they chose to experience that love through sexuality within a physical body.*

This is a very important factor that is rarely raised, yet is one of the reasons we often battle to find unconditional love for ourselves and others, because it has proved to be such a challenge to all beings on Earth, at one time or another.

In the beginning, when the first civilizations were formed, the original one in **Elysium** mainly consisted of volunteers from other galaxies and star systems, in both *male and female* bodies, which presented no problems.

However in the lands of *Lemuria,* the experiment was to live life here in **androgynous form,** so male and female were in *one body.*

All went wonderfully well, and Lemurians essentially lived in peace, creating new forms of plant and animal life. That was until the rise of *Atlantis,* on the other side of the planet, in those lands where the Atlantic Ocean now is. Masculine and feminine, once again had separate identities, and so there was physical sex between the male and female bodies, which the Lemurians could not experience in their androgynous form! Some felt they were losing out on something vital, and so apparently enjoyable, that a group of scientists came up with the idea of separating them into male and female aspects, to create two bodies from the androgynous form!

Now those souls who decided to have this operation (for they underwent a surgical procedure separating them into two distinctive forms) had to sign a **Soul Contract**, acknowledging that this was taking place merely for them to experience what it felt like for a soul to have a separate male and female aspect (note – it was only *Lemurians* who did this – not *Atlanteans*, who already had male and female bodies). So in reality what these souls wished to experience, was sexual love and union, – the coming together of male and female parts in the sexual act for procreation (in those days) for a certain *power that was emitted during the sexual act* – this is very important to understand!

When signing this *Soul Contract*, they also specified that their souls chose to experience life in two separate forms (which their souls had not originally been created for, as creation has three distinctive birthing forms – *male, female or androgynous*. So this was an aspect which their souls forfeited, the experience of life in an androgynous form. Those who signed did so with the full knowledge that they could not return to the androgynous form once parted).

The moment this separation occurred, (one soul

splitting to accommodate two forms), it ushered in a crisis to *Lemuria*, as suddenly disputes and unhappiness resulted *between two souls who had previously been one and the same.* This which was totally foreign to them, and ultimately was one of the reasons why *Lemuria* lost its identity and eventually sank into the sea.

Suddenly males and females found that they loved the act of sex, and when the first delight in each other wore off (the novelty of having sex), they started looking at others, searching to once more find that spark they had experienced in their first union of the two halves, This resulted in the division between the two becoming greater and more pronounced, and eventually, most of the *Lemurians* who had agreed to this, found their lives hanging in limbo. For somehow they did not belong amongst their people any more, and due to their distinct and different physical form (which was originally in 7th dimension, whilst the *Atlanteans* were 5th dimensional beings) they did not fit in with the *Atlanteans either.* Most significantly, for the first time they experienced loneliness and separation from the other half of themselves, their own soul(s).

Through this feeling of alienation from self and others, they also experienced separation from the Divine Source.

From this moment onwards humanity has had to experience this repeatedly, until they could learn to **step past illusion** and into wholeness and oneness once more.

Treasures of the Heart

I gather close the treasures…
True treasures of the heart….
Close to me I gather,
The people that I love…
And in my precious gallery
They make light a thousand paths…
A thousand petals gathered,
Amongst the sacred
Halls of Wisdom…..
And books,
Rare and profound…
The others were the teachers
Mentors
Souls,
So manifold……
I gather close the treasures
The treasures of my heart
Life is taking on a new form…

It is there is in the heart centre, the heart space, and in the way our hearts are opening more and more to love… The greater *cosmic whole* is holding its breath, as they are here to assist this whole process and then to bring us into alignment with our own higher soul selves and our latent abilities and soul attributes, and gifts which will now truly come to the fore….

Love is an alchemical dance

It perches on the brink
You mix all the ingredients
to turn the lead
To gold…..
Yet strangely all it
Does –
it lead you
Back
To self……
For only in embracing self
Wholeheartedly
Does that
Embrace
Expand, expand
To include
Within its great
swirling dance
The other's
Wholeness….
Paradox
Lies in the opposites
Converging
Within spaces
Where blending is
Allowed –

Then swirling ever out
Once more
Until the dance
Assumes
The first
Again......

Judith Küsel

Chapter 7

Musings on Marriage, Twin flames, Soul Mates

I was asked a simple question yesterday, and it set me thinking, musing – a deep and profound reflection....

Since I started my ***Twin Flame* Soul Readings**, (a friend prompted me to do them over and above my normal soul readings, and they are now in even greater demand), I have found most people come for guidance. They feel deep down that they have met *the one and only*, and now wish to make sure and know a bit more. Others just want to know if they will ever meet the *One*.

During recent years, (I started these readings in 2012), I have found certain patterns emerging during these sessions, and I want to elaborate on this. I have been reflecting deeply, and searching for answers from my innermost being, since meeting my own *Twin Flame* a few years ago.

1. Within each S*oul Group* there are *144 souls* (some Soul Groups combine under a *Cosmic Soul Group*, which consists of 144, 000 souls who collectively work on the same vibrational frequencies. These large groups are those very

old souls, birthed at the very beginning of Creation, forming part of the **12 Sons and Daughters** of the Most High. Each one of the 12 make up the Elders around the Throne of God, and therefore each of the first 12 Galaxies born at the very beginning, have one of the sons and daughters in charge of that Galaxy. (This however, is a story for another time.)

2. Your soul consists of 12 sparks, or flames (vibrational frequency – that is why your *soul name, galaxy of origin, tonal chord* and *soul colors* will be that pure vibrational frequency). This is the *unique* frequency of you, and you will only be in true harmony with yourself, if your vibration stays at that frequency. However, in this lifetime in 99% of cases, two of these flames or sparks, at the most have incarnated. Those groups of souls, however, who have been involved with the creation of Earth from its origin (they hail from the original Galaxies involved here, forming part of the original 12), all have 12 flames incarnated at this time, for *Higher Service to humanity,* on a special mission. This entails the completion of karmic ties with Earth, as they now wish to move on to a higher state of evolutionary being, with the rest of their *Soul Group. (Creation is always evolving, growing and becoming, and so are soul groups and souls. As one soul forms part of the whole soul group, even a single soul who is not able to end the cycle, holds up the rest of that group. The collective will*

*always aid this soul until it manages to fulfill its
calling, and as such no one is ever separated or
excluded from their group, for it is eternally part of
that group).*

3. Not all *Twin Flames* have incarnated. In those
cases where only one flame has, they will have
the constant support of all the other 11 flames,
and are reunited with them during sleep state.
They will then act as higher guides for this soul
during its incarnation.

4. Some of the *Indigo, Crystal, Rainbow* and *Sun
children* stem from new Galaxies, which were
not involved with Earth from its origins. They
are here as volunteer souls, and therefore have
no karmic links here. Most will *not* have a twin
flame incarnated, yet will have *Soul Mates* here,
as spiritual support, and will recognize and have
an affinity with those from the same galaxies as
themselves. Autistic children fall very much in
this category, because they are often highly
evolved souls, and may have great difficulty
communicating what is deep inside of them,
not having previously been familiar with speech
(they use telepathy) and never having
encountered violence in any form.

I feel this needs to be clarified, for we often make
ourselves miserable searching for *The One*. Due to the
current *Twin Flame* hype on the Internet etc. some
souls feel they are missing the boat, but when understanding dawns, it can open up other possibilities in

relationships, which always brings one back to the Heart of Love and most importantly, **to self–love**.

Most souls incarnated here now, apart from those mentioned above, have had karmic links with Earth for millions of years. At the very beginning when the planet was newly born and bliss and harmony reigned, men and women loved each other with no disharmony. At the dawn of these galaxies, they were involved in creation, and began the experiment here with no problems. They merely carried on, as they had always done in their home galaxies and on their Motherships.

However, during the course of Earth's creation, something went dreadfully awry. (I will not tell the whole story here, for that is part of my book '**Why I was born In Africa**'). Certain *patterns* were created between souls (not always *Twin Flames* and *Soul Mates*, but also with souls from other soul groups), which became destructive and completely shattered the old order.

In *Mu* and then *Lemuria*, another karmic pattern made itself felt, which left these souls struggling with the same karmic link. The souls born into both these civilizations incarnated into the 7th *dimensional state* and were **androgynous**! All went perfectly well, until 5th *dimensional Atlantis* arose, and in this experiment with the 6th *root race* on the planet, there were male and female beings in two separate forms. Those from *Mu* and *Lemuria* suddenly felt they were missing out on t*he mating game!*

The *Lemurian* High Priesthood invented a surgical method in which they split the androgynous form into two – a masculine and a feminine form! This experiment seemed to work for a short time, but gave way to deep seated unhappiness, and a search for the unity and oneness that had been experienced before the split. One day the two split halves came to understand that they had lost something of the intimacy, the closeness – the *oneness of the androgynous* form, and most importantly the balance.

So then, what is happening to the souls currently incarnated on Earth, who have karmic links from these ancient civilizations?

1. Old Karmic Patterns between two souls need to be resolved once and for all. The crux of the matter is that once a pattern had been created, it repeated itself, and some souls have the same old patterns repeating over many lifetimes. So, they will be drawn together again in this lifetime, until that pattern is finally dissolved, and a new one created. This forms part and particle of *soul contract lessons.*

2. *Marriage vows, blood vows, rituals.* Originally there was no need to formalize any unions. During the long history of this Earth however, some warped thinking came into play, involving *control and possession.* Most often women became a bargaining tool. When land and dowries became essential, they often became pawns in the power play of men and they were ill-treated as chattels. In times of war men were killed, and the conquerors raped the

enemy in order to beget more offspring (to enslave) and women were either enslaved or shipped into harems and used as concubines (depending on their assets).

In the case where blood vows were made, another factor was added, for this formed an immensely strong tie, lasting over many lifetimes, if not undone. These likewise were not always made in love, but rather to knit tribes together, or to force treaties to be honored.

Now as the old makes way for the new, we cannot afford to carry those old patterns into the new era. So we will be challenged to dissolve them so that our *collective consciousness* is freed to move into a new and higher awareness. Here the law of the *One and the Many* comes into effect. Even one couple dissolving a pattern has a ripple effect on others. Likewise even one couple creating a new, balanced pattern has a similar beneficial ripple effect on all others. What happens to one then happens to many.

All of us have numerous and varied links to different souls, and before incarnating, those still karmically connected to us, will be contracted to meet us again, at one time or another, in this lifetime.

In the case of *Twin Flames* for instance, each one may have karmic links from other lifetimes to first work through, before they can meet here and now. Often when they do meet, one twin is still working through those ties, and therefore is not free, or not ready for the intensity of such a union. It could also be that the two have created karmic patterns over many lifetimes, which first have to be cleared, before true union can be attained. With *Twin Flames*, it is necessary to understand that each flame has to be of the same potency – otherwise one will "consume" the other and imbalance will occur.

If you consider how many souls you have met here, in **one** single lifetime, then you will start to appreciate that we are in relationship with every single person we meet every day, whether intimately or not.

I am aware that we are all essentially **One;** stemming from **One** *and the same Source,* and in the greater Cosmic whole, form part of *One single whole. Thus* I am responsible for my own life and my actions and re-actions to everyone I come into contact with. You can never bypass the cosmic law of *Cause and Effect. If we observe any particle, when even a small piece of it breaks away*, this has an effect on the greater whole – like one drop of water sending out ripple effects. So imagine yourself sending out oscillating waves of energy, through all you are and do in every moment. Now multiply that by many lifetimes, and see what happens, – you become a vibrant catalyst, that is how powerful you are in reality!

So in every lifetime you've had, your existence was a catalyst in some form or other. You need not have been a King or Queen of a country, to have effected huge change within your own sphere of influence. As you lived, you created patterns which we shall examine further.

In his book[5] *"Fractal Time"* **Gregg Braden** examines the aspects of destructive patterns, created over thousands of years. In conclusion he gives the example of a kaleidoscope, which has a pattern which remains the same, until the lens is turned, and the pieces dissolve into a scrambled mess, before forming a new pattern. He states that the greatest lesson to master on Earth, is to create a new consciousness and way of living on multiple levels.

In your life now you will attract souls with whom you have karmic patterns to clear, whether ties of love or hate. They arrive in the form of family, friends, enemies or lovers, or even spouses, but the pattern will be obvious, and if destructive will remain until you learn to dissolve and release it. In that moment of letting go, a vacuum is created, and in it a new pattern forms.

So the more one does the inner clearing, the stronger the vacuum, enabling a new way of loving and living to emerge.

We needs to balance our own inner understanding of what love and commitment are. I cannot do that for you. No one else can, as it is personal work. Each soul has to do this, by digging deep and deeper into its own *inner being*, heart and soul.

I have been doing this for many long years, and every time I think a pattern is dissolved, up comes the

---

[5] *"Fractal Time"* **Gregg Braden** The Secret of 2012 and a New World Age. Greg Braden's sixth book on the theme of putting god and science back in bed together, endeavors to reveal the mathematics of the cyclical nature of events.

next one, and then the next! The understanding is dawning that I have been a *catalyst* in all my incarnations on Earth. Thus, as I am here to anchor in the *New Golden Age*, and to become one of its *co-creators,* I have to practice what I preach. I cannot lead others, if I am not prepared to first do the inner work on myself.

Deep down all of us have a profound inner wish, to be loved and accepted for who and what we are!

However, most of us have great difficulty in truly practicing self-love. We are hardest on ourselves. Until we learn the lesson of loving and accepting ourselves on all levels – physical, emotional, and mental, we will have challenges in our relationships.

Notice that I am not speaking of romance here, but rather of *worthiness and love.*

Of course when we are in love we wish to give to our partner, and make them happy – that is natural, and is a subject for another time. I am one of the most romantic people there is: I dreamt of marriage, my Knight in Shining Armor sweeping me off my feet, etc. I own that.

Your Soul Name and Soul Group Name will always reflect that the soul is here first and foremost to **serve** *in whatever form and capacity that is required.* For example: My soul name: **The Shining One Who Exalts.** My Soul Group Name; The **Illumined Ones**, also known as **The Shining Ones** and **The Ancient Ones**. My given name Judith – **She who is a praise to the Lord**, my middle name: Alida – **The Noble One**, and my Surname: **The Gentle One** (German word gemütlich). See how all of that ties in together. My soul group has been involved with this planet even before its creation, and we are here now to see our work to completion. I am primarily here to **serve,** *by becoming, bringing in and transmitting what my Soul Name reflects.*

A Soul is created first and foremost to reflect a trait, or aspect of the Divine Source back to Itself – so that the Divine may experience life in multiple forms through its own Creation! You were created to reflect a part of God back to God, so that God can experience Its Divine Creation through you!!

I was asked recently if I would accept if I received a marriage proposal.

Here is my honest answer: As a teenager I devoured Mills & Boon Romances, with profound dreams of my *Twin Flame.* All I wanted to do, was to follow the example of all my extended family members, (multiple cousins and friends) find a man to marry as soon as possible, settle down and have a family. Well, instead life has led me down another path all together, and it is only in recent years, after much soul searching that I finally understood that karmic patterns, and what had occurred in a past life (after meeting my twin), had led to me not marrying this lifetime. As memory bank after memory bank triggered, and I had to release pattern after pattern, I started to heal these deep soul wounds gathered over many lifetimes. I finally understood the whole concept of loving and accepting myself first of all, before I could be able to totally love and accept another – warts and all.

I believe I have finally grown up!

I also understand, that my own life's calling and the completion of my soul mission is of vital importance. This is what gives meaning and purpose to my life and I am here to serve the greater *Cosmic All*. This is not about me, it never has been. It is about serving the Greater All. That is first and foremost why I am here now. No one else can live my life for me. I am mastering my own life and taking responsibility for my soul, and for my actions and reactions.

Marriage?

Yes, if I felt a deep love, respect, and honor for the man I love, and if we were on the same wavelength/frequency band, I certainly would consider it. That doesn't mean that there would not be challenges, for in many ways we would be similar, but also complete opposites, as you can only create balance and bliss if both polarities are there. Most importantly, *if his sense of mission, vision, and quest for higher service to humanity matched mine, and our union could became a total and utter dedication to serving the Higher purpose, then I would say yes!*

I will add that if, no matter what happened, that shared vision could pull us through the good and bad times, then yes!

Deep down I believe that any true and profound union has many levels of experiencing the Divine through living it in every moment. In such a union there has to always be a third energy involved and that is t*he Divine flame of love, power and wisdom*. Without that, no union can ever be complete.

I leave you with your own musings ....

I merely wished to add to your awareness....

I am learning to travel the higher pathways of love.

Like a budding rose opening up petal by petal...
And just allowing whatever comes....
For it is an unfolding within itself.
Perhaps the why's, the hows, the how-come
have all been blown away....
as dry leaves are blown away by the wind –
and then trust has returned
that whatever life brings,
Love will soar and fly and win through it all!
It always has –
It always will –
It always shines through in the end: –
For love
Loves
Ad infinitum....
and I want to savor each moment,
each precious minute of Being
the eternal ebb and the flow...
where two Rivers of life
flow into ONE
and become the very River of Life
flowing into the Eternal Ocean of Love.
Just a deep simplicity dawning upon me this

morning..

The simple – the profound.

All truth at its core is very simple.

All Universal Laws at their very core are very simple.

So I jotted down the following in my diary for it speaks from my soul:

Just immense, intense LOVE!

Just want to love, love, love!

Receiving love.

Giving Love.

Being LOVE.

That's all!

Nothing else.

Plain and simple.

And somewhere in the mists of time

Love becomes BEING

and interestingly

has always been: –

SIMPLICITY…

Judith Küsel

FEMININE DIVINE

Chapter 8

The Quantum Shift in Relationships – the Return to True Love

There is a deep and profound shift taking place in the human heart right now, not only in the individual, but also on the Earth and in the Cosmos, as everything is linked.

It is the Eternal Flame of the heart, and thus the highest frequency there is, for *"it is only with the heart that one can see clearly. What is essential is invisible to the eye!"*[6]

I feel society's ideas of relationships need a massive transformation, from the old Edwardian idea of marriage, which our ancestral lines established in the 1900's. These notions fell apart at the seams in less than one hundred years, as new lifestyles started forming, bringing in the concept of greater freedom and equal opportunity for women, with a more relaxed acceptance of couples living together without a commitment, and no legal agreements, but this too was

---

[6] Antoine de St. Exupery, The Little Prince Written in wartime New York City, the children's book brings out the small explorer in everyone. Antoine de Saint-Exupéry (1900–1944).

just an illusion.

For even when the old ways seemed to fall apart, the world still believed in a freedom, allowing sex with all and sundry, and so the demand grew for a more ideal sexual partner. Yet, even that concept started losing its appeal, as one partner after the other came and went, and the inner void loomed larger and larger. You can never develop true relationship or intimacy in one-night stands, and the heart is not engaged unless the sexual relationship comes forth from the sacred heart space. Sex may be an excellent form of gymnastics, but it does not always connect to the heart and thus the very Life-force itself! Orgasms deplete the life-force, if released outwards, and cannot become the sacred energy force they were meant to be.

During these last few years, I have counseled many clients, mostly women, who in private moments, confided that they felt they were being used by men as an instrument for relief through sex, and were not being honored at a deep soul level, in the man's heart space, but rather for "ego" and mere physical gratification. Women may do this too, but it is usually they who feel this lack of emotional connection, as they tend to operate more from the heart in not speaking up about what has really exacerbated the situation.

Some men have been behaving badly in the area of bonding, sharing love, and showing limited understanding of the true meaning of sexual union and sexual energy, which has caused a total relationship collapse, and consequently, has ushered in real change for us all. Without all the chaos and breakdowns happening, we could not evolve.

In many ways it is ironic, that the downfall of humanity took place when we first discovered the power of sex. The upward movement to higher states of consciousness cannot truly happen, until we learn that we cannot abuse or misuse certain energies, without causing serious repercussions. Nowhere is this more apparent than in the arena of sexual energy.

There is an ancient core truth here, purposefully long hidden from humankind, which will not reveal itself, until the seeker is really ready to find answers to their own sexuality. They must be willing to find the *higher road* and state of being, and only engage sexually with the correct partner, who honors the sacred, and shares the same path.

There is a much loftier reason for this, which was lost in the mists of amnesia, so everyone incarnated on Earth will suffer in consequence.

It all hinges on that first *union,* between the masculine and the feminine Divine, *two equal parts – just two equal circles* forming a union, which shifts into a third, and from that creative force, the fourth is born.

The *Divine Feminine* is the receptive part, the one who gracefully, gratefully and with immense Love opens her sacred areas, those treasured parts of her energy base, for her full powerbase resides in her sexual area. Thus, if she truly feels loved, honored and respected for her deep inner core heart and soul identity, she will not only receive openly, lovingly and generously, but she will give back in equal measure with all of her being. He in turn brings the life-penetrating, life giving force, and in the act of union, giver and receiver become as one in an equal exchange of higher energy. This energy forms a *vortex* – *w*hich is a creative force, and the third component.

However, unions that are just for self-satisfaction, self-service or gratification, become a destructive force.

The Ego continually wants to be acknowledged, to be petted and reminded how wonderful it is. The heart knows however, that there is no place for this ego in a truly loving and complete union, which comes from the heart, connects to the heart and then flows from the heart.

There is a key difference here to be taken note of.

Firstly, if the heart-space is not fully empowered and open, whatever the body does or doesn't do, is irrelevant to its energy force. The body can only expand its energy, if the heart and body are engaged as a *single force*. Additionally, the mind must be in harmony with the spirit, for all bodies are intertwined with the auric energy field beyond it.

Ancient Ones knew this, so if two people desired union to procreate, they read their auras, soul records and energy fields. They knew that if one or the other was out of sync, and the heart intention were from different spheres, then a true loving union could not manifest.

To me, this makes a lot of sense. If, for instance Mary Magdalene, had not been on the same energy level as the Christed energy of Yeshua, neither of them could have had a true union with the other. The Christed energy flows from the heart space and so, when two equal units meet and merge, then a miracle occurs as they expand in union to form a totally new energy field, which is the *quantum field,* connecting to the *super quantum field,* which is the energy field of all existence!

So it may perhaps be wiser to refrain from a premature pairing, rather waiting, until both reach a point where there is just love, in a higher conscious loving state.

We can learn to use orgasms in the correct way to expand infinitely into the creative energy force, so as not to diminish the Divine energy. *This sacred sexual energy is the highest form of energy there is.*

More than this, it has to do with the matching of souls, and the conscious vibrational frequencies of souls joining together. When equally matched, it is the most beautifully amazing and precious union there can ever be, and one that is sanctified far and wide.

This is true union, with so much loving, tender and heartfelt love, that honors the beauty of the soul in the other, and is reflected in every single cell, sinew and vibration of the physical form, the body's auric field, and most of all, the union of true minds and spirits.

We cannot have this with just anyone! There lies the secret. It is wise to honor the sacredness of your soul, and your sexuality as an entrance point into unlocking the full potential of this union. Once understanding dawns, you will seek nothing less than the ultimate relationship, which is the most blessed holy union.

If we have lost respect for our own soul's immense

and powerful energies, we can equally lose respect for others we may seek to merge with. Once our hearts change, we change from our inner core, and are seen for who we really are. Then we are able to recognize who most clearly reflects the same vibrational state of being. Then, and only then, may our sacred union occur, in the spirit of profound respect and honor.

Many people are stressing about the return of the *Divine Feminine*, but it must be remembered, that essentially this is about unconditional love and acceptance. Yes, men did awful things to women – raped, and abused them and so on. Often they were totally helpless, but let us never forget that some women serve in the armies of the world, and are anything but gentle, nurturing and kind. For instance, I know for a fact that some armies use women to train their crack troops, for they can have less mercy than men, here lies the shadow which we have to embrace!

Instead of blaming men for all the woes on this planet, we could learn compassion and unconditional love and acceptance. If women could learn to take men deep inside, in order to teach them love, and create beautiful music together, to soothe the hurts and pain, this could bring us all into the higher state of consciousness, where the male and female aspects of life are beautifully balanced, and we are all at peace.

Love for me
means a willingness to open up to you
And to let you in,

Deep into the inner sanctuaries
Of my heart, body, mind, spirit and soul...
Sometimes it feels a little scary
For I am not used to letting someone in
That close...
Then I tend to want to shrink away
And simply get at peace with this once more...
Then I find myself listening for your heart
Your soul, the inner promptings of your spirit
And long for the wisdom of your mind...

I smile when I remember a million kisses
Dancing on my naked skin...
And the amazing wonders of your tongue
Finding the epicentres
Transporting vortexes of energies combined....
I smile...
Then I open up my arms once more and simply
let you in...
For I just wish to lie, to be with you,
Feel myself sheltered in your arms...
at home....
That's where I truly WISH to be...
In the sacred sanctuary of you and me....

Judith Küsel

Chapter 9

The Celebration of Love…

Love at its very nucleus adores to be celebrated, for it exudes joy, bliss and an infinite euphoria, from the coming together of the masculine and feminine God and Goddess, within and without.

There is an adoration of the Divine within each partner, reflected in the eyes of the *Beloved*. It is the depth of the mystery of love itself, mirrored in the other's eyes, in the *depth of soul* revealed.

Love is best shown by two souls who have known each other from the outset, inside and out, issuing forth, conceived by the Goddess, and birthed as one. Two souls who have traversed many galaxies, star systems, dimensions and life forms with parallel existences. With such a soul self, there is no division, no separateness, for the soul is **At–one.**

We are in a totally new paradigm shift, already making itself felt, and at this time souls destined to be together will truly join together to do more important

work:[7] "*Love is not so much gazing at each other, but looking **outward into the same direction**.*"

As much as you celebrate the Beloved, and are delving the depths and exploring, celebrating the infinite pleasures of coming together at this momentous time, it is also that outward fusion, **as one,** that must now serve humanity and our Earth. For such souls have excelled in performing as one, all over the Cosmos, and have incarnated at this time to work as one, in order to help Earth move through the immense shift currently taking place.

This is a common bond, a common Quest, which ties these two souls together, acting in higher service and celebrating the new beginnings of life on Earth.

Devotion to a beloved can assume different forms and expressions. Adoration should not just be there in moments when we celebrate being loved and loving, but also in challenging times. Obstacles in life are an integral and agreed upon part of being here, to fine tune our inner strength and resilience, just as shared love does. When challenged, it is time to delve deep within, and find that which one has truly always adored, loved, admired, and celebrated in the beloved.

When the positives outweigh the negatives, then we are inspired to move into the higher octaves of being, which motivate us to return to our point of equilibrium, as there we find this balance and see that both parts are needed for completion, to bring us ever closer together, almost in spite of

---

[7] Antoine de St. Exupery, The Little Prince Written in wartime New York City, the children's book brings out the small explorer in everyone. Antoine de Saint-Exupéry (1900–1944).

ourselves.

The celebration of love and the beloved, includes acknowledging your vulnerability, insecurities, fears, everything that makes you who you are, and includes all past lives, parallel lives, existences, in any dimension in the Cosmos. Many of those inherent fears come from past life memory banks, which may be triggered time and again.

This concerns the *higher healing of the soul wounds from Atlantis,* and what went before.

I have had discussions with many women recently who are feeling this shift intensely as it literally opens them to their core. It is there hidden in our emotional bodies, within each vertebrae of the spinal column, in the root, sacral, solar plexus and throat chakras. It is confronting those memory banks which reveal the *unspeakable acts* which happened to so many of us in other lifetimes here, and even in the present one.

Our throat chakras were obstructed due to being silenced, our voices could not be heard anymore as humanity sunk into insanity and imbalance, as men retreated totally into their minds, trying to exclude their hearts, and attempting to completely **disown** the feminine, including their own feminine side.

Women were persecuted for their psychic abilities, inner knowing, deep seeing, and for their knowledge. They held incredibly powerful planetary, cosmic keys and codes in the *High Priesthood,* in the *Wise Women Shamanic Lineage.* In Druidic tradition women held all the powers of transmitting knowledge, of prophecy and also retained the power of the oracles, as well as the energy (still hidden) on Earth. They were not only powerful healers with these inherent powers, but they worked with the crystal kingdom, the elementals, the devas, and Mother Earth, in ways that men could not understand. They could access these powers because of their intimate links through their womb and yoni, to the same energies in Mother Earth. There is an immense mystery in the deepest parts of the womb, which are incredibly powerful and which we have not even begun to access yet.

In Atlantis the soul was removed from women. They were treated as objects, as if they were beings devoid of spirit and emotions, soul-less and feeling-less.

As these far reaching changes are occurring, women, must begin to celebrate their womanhood again, and not to aspire to be like men. There truly is no need for competition!

*Women must remember how to celebrate their woman-hood, their womb, and sacred power centers, as the very essence of what makes a woman. There are **7 Gateways of Womanhood** held within the yoni, and therefore 7 gateways to the womb. The pelvic bowl is a massive energy center, and until women learn to reconnect with this immense power base, and to celebrate this to the fullest, healing their immense soul scars, they cannot truly be open to appreciating men or to celebrating love in its expansive form.*

At this time, all those ancient memories from *Atlantis* and previous life events, will begin to feel more real and indeed in some women these have already triggered recently, especially since 2004.

Women need to reconnect with their *souls for it was*

the soul in womanhood which was denied in Atlantis. A woman in touch with her soul, and living her soul purpose and calling, while feeling in sync with her womb, cannot do other than celebrate her womanhood. The ancient wise women knew the yoni/womb was connected to the yoni of the Earth, and therefore all women's psychic abilities open up ten thousand fold, when fully grounded into Mother Earth.

An awakened woman who has found her root voice is vibrant, alive and celebrates her life, for she is a **custodian** and **giver of life.** The fact is that all Creation celebrates the holy **balance** between masculine and feminine. The one cannot fully function without the other.

The celebration of the beloved must first be in essence, a celebration of yourself and everything that makes you who you are. However this goes much deeper – it is essentially the celebration of the Life force itself, and the soul. Then we may open ourselves totally to the core, in the adoration and celebration of our beloved and therefore:

Soul meets soul.
Heart meets heart.
Spirit meets spirit.
Higher mind meets higher mind.
Feelings meet feelings.
Body meets body.

All of these make up a man and woman. Not one iota is ever missing. All is perfection in motion.

To celebrate the Beloved, is to truly adore him or her. It is a deep **trust, respect, a love** which is not earthbound – it is **cosmic.** For it expands beyond any limitations of this earthly existence into **infinite space where souls are birthed and exist as one entity.**

When soul meets soul, there is such a deep, intense and profound connection, which lights up the cosmic fire in both of them.

To meet the beloved with an open heart, body, mind, spirit and soul, is to embrace wholeness within and without. There are no limitations. You expands into the state of dissolving. You dissolves into the state of infinite bliss – the cosmic orgasm which created life itself.

A conscious awareness – a state of sublime consciousness which holds both the Earth and the Cosmos at the core, celebrating both the finite and infinite.

Man dissolves from the finite, into the infinite.

Woman dissolves from the finite, into the Infinite.

WE dissolve from the finite – into the Infinite.

When infinite space moves into the finite – enlightenment occurs, for the cosmic fire within each of them ignites into one single three-fold flame/fire.

The celebration of life, of love, of consciousness then becomes the adoration itself. All flows into a single cosmic stream – the same stream of life which is Creation itself.

Such is the gift of this time we are entering into.

When all the mess, the pain, the trauma of Atlantis and the thousands of years when women were considered soulless, finally is laid to rest, men and women will return to the original state of the Garden of Eden – in balance, harmony and simple adoration of each other.

Such is the gift!

If I had a paintbrush

If I had a paintbrush
And you were the canvas
I would dabble you
With bright colours
And hues
That reflect the magnificence
Of a far greater
Master hand....
I would sprinkle in joy,
Laughter
And bliss...
I would add waterfalls,
Fountains,
Roses and lilies...
Playing in luscious
Green valleys and hills.....
And let you lie
In the cushions
Of grass on the banks.....
In the fragrance.....
Breathing in
The life-giving
Force
Of ALL-THAT-IS....
I would become one

With you
In a myriad of ways
So that
You drink from
The very fountains
Of my heart and my soul….
This strengthen
You
To walk majestically
Tall
Like the Oak
clad in its glorious
Summer cloak….

In the fountains
Of my heart….
There is
Just YOU ……..
We are one and the same
I AM YOU!!!!

Judith Küsel

Chapter 10

Letting go

Women are having to learn to keep their hearts open during this time, and to love, despite whatever confusion is being shown to them, in so many forms.

This is not true just for women, but also, of course for men, however I am specifically speaking to women here, for I deal primarily with them, through the services I offer. Women have often been left to rear the children when men abandon them, or they bear the brunt of this duty, when, in the case of divorce, some men refuse to pay alimony or child support, for example. This leaves indelible scars on some which can turn into bitterness and anger, and a deep-seated distrust of men.

The challenge now is to release all of that, as it no longer serves our highest good. We don't have to judge the right or the wrong of any situation, but merely trust our inner knowing that somehow all experiences were called into being as part of our path, and have taken place so older ways of relating could dissolve, and the new could step in. Perhaps the greatest lesson for women is to first find love for themselves, in the deepest sense to find their own completion from within. No man will ever be able to do this in place of us, it is something we need to discover.

As the new is forming, with balance returning, fresh ways will be revealed, and we will learn to be more discerning about who we allow into our energy fields, to share our inner sanctuaries. We will practice making the distinction between lust and true love, knowing when we truly honor the temples of our own bodies and souls, we will only allow partners in, who are also able to honor our space.

Nobody hurts another intentionally, but because they themselves are feeling pain and a void inside. Is it not true that we often hit out at those we are closest to?

Sometimes two people have merely outlived their *togetherness*, and the lessons they had to master, and now, with the lessons learnt, they need to move on to greater ones.

Instead of trying to cage someone in, s*et them free*. Once they are free to fly and if your love is true, they will return to you, and may even alight on your shoulder one day with more and greater love, than ever before! Yes, give them the freedom to explore and to be – and give yourself this freedom as well.

There has been a dramatic shift with the opening up of the Earth's heart centres and of amazingly potent new energies, in a vast forward thrust.

Yet, at the same time, these are *Divine Feminine energies*, and thus have a vulnerability about them, which always comes with the true opening up of the heart. In those first moments, love for another makes us open the secret and sacred places of our hearts, that inner sanctuary into which we only allow those who we truly trust.

This is gentle, yet so very sensitive, so vulnerable, fragile but strong, – it is the opening up of the very core of the most exquisite rose.

So often we wish for dramatic life changes, and then, when they come, they seem like a tidal wave hitting us, when in truth we have been prepared for this moment all along.

So expect things to start moving and changing as you open your heart centre more and more, expect the old to simply fall away, and find that the new seems to sprout from thin air, and blossom in the most amazing spring-time of your life.

We are being brought back to the heart, back to feelings, back to the very womb of the Mother, and safely cradled there in her innermost self, we are being reborn into the inner sacred sanctuary of the heart energies that stem from the Great Mother herself.

It is here that we start relearning to become *as One* with everything else, with the Earth and the Sky, the Cosmic Heaven above; the innermost sacred centres and spaces of Mother Earth. The Magnetic pull from our heart reconnects us with the magnetic heart of Gaia, and with it, the epicentre of all life in and on Earth.

Here we expand into something greater than we can even comprehend.

So many of us have had to leave many aspects of self behind us, and often seemed to lose so much in the process, as all started falling away. We have shed skin after skin, and we were opened up to the core of our very sensitive and vulnerable selves.

Yet, at the same time, we have found that inner strength and inner resilience, which we would never have found, if all this had not happened – we have found the pure gold mines deep within ourselves.

We are like the rarest and most precious of diamonds, honed and nurtured into *beingness* deep within Mother Earth, formed from the severest pressure, simply sparkling and shining beyond anything found here on Earth. We have lost it all, yet have found ourselves, and beyond that our infinite connection to the Divine. We have shrunk, and then expanded until we are infinitely more beautiful and more exquisite souls than ever before.

Now, we are being pulled into action, we are asked to bring these beautiful soul gifts to the world. We are asked to render the Highest Service, – to simply do this from the heart, and to let love overflow.

We are asked to heal Mother Earth by learning to nurture her heart and her soul, and to send healing energies from our heart centre into hers.

We are asked to simply allow ourselves to be used, by the loving hands of the Mother, who whispers her love and who holds us in her womb and her heart.

This Flame of Love, burning inside us and extending from our own inner core, will not only light up our own lives, but also the world and even beyond.

New Life has sprung into Cosmic Beingness.

Rejoice! The Time of the great Age has begun!

At this moment in time the cosmic energies of the heart are flowing in us and through us with great force.

The minute we ask for assistance to let go of old baggage and pain, that assistance will come, and we will be liberated to move on, and to feel lighter, happier and freer in multiple ways.

To me the whole heart opening is a process of becoming freer and more able to express what is deep inside of me, and to know, it's okay!

I AM THAT

Thou art THAT
All of this is nothing but THAT
And that alone is!
We are but
Double Helix strands
Of purest energy...
We have forgotten who we are...
As mists veil us in time....
Yet... slowly... surely...
The 7th Sun...
Is rising once again...
And suddenly...
The veil will lift...
The Seeing returned...
And there we are...
At last...
Seen!
Pure Beings of pure Light!

All curves
All curves... all woman... all wanton...

am I…

Have been since the beginning of time…

Exuberant blossoming

Sensuous unfolding…..

Intricate sensations…

Expressions expressing……

Euphoric enticement……

Blending hues of

Aphrodite, Freya, Isis and Venus…

The Goddesses celebrate me….

I am the LOVE

Of a thousand ways

I am the JOY

Each dawn brings

I am the Promise

Magically spun by the moon

And dancing amongst

The star-studded realms

Of the Other-worlds

And those within…

I am wise…

I am knowing…

I am all woman…

All woman…

I'm ME!

Judith Küsel

Chapter 11

The Bride is ready

The Divine Mother is back!

Her power is love, her sword is Light and she brings immense and powerful creative energies. Whatever she touches she fills with the spirit and soul of rebirth and renewal. She sweeps through the pelvic bowl of the Earth Mother, and she is renewing the life giving forces.

She is penetrating the shields of destruction. She is opening the heart and soul of humanity. She is assisted by the Cosmic Forces gathered around the planet, who help her by beaming in powerful light. She is penetrating each cell and DNA strand of all bodies. She is activating the portals and grids. She is sending her hand-picked maidens to open these portals and grids; to bring the crystal chambers into action, and once again to activate the Web of Light.

She is sending her female representatives into all four corners of the Earth. She is rallying them forth. She is bringing the Ancient Wisdom and Knowledge back to this planet. She is sweeping clean the debris, war and destruction; she is cleaning the oceans, the mountains, rivers and streams. She is sweeping the air of all pollution; she is bringing in the children who will rule the new planet, birthed from the death-throws of the old.

Her touch is gentle and her heart filled with love. For her Love is unconditional, knowing that even the darkness fears the Light. Thus it served the purpose of showing all souls what darkness is, when we are not in perfect balance with the Light, for darkness reflects the light and makes it shine all the brighter.

She embraces the masculine. She is awakening the feminine powers within the masculine, and bringing this into balance once more. She embraces the male, for she has to have his power, his manhood filling her womb with the seed of his love, in order to truly create the new.

They are dancing the tango, the beautiful dance of love and light, when in perfect harmony and balance. Then all is a dance of creation, and everything is one with Creation. One is never more than the other – simply a beautiful balance between dark and light, masculine and feminine.

She is bringing the *New Golden Age*. She is gathering all her women and maidens and preparing them for their feminine powers to blend beautifully with the masculine, – to teach men the art of an open heart and the power of Love.

She is returning the *Ancient Sexual Rites* (which had been forgotten – and mal-practiced by certain cults, who only used a part of the potent feminine power). She has hand-picked her maidens, identifying and training them personally. They are the ones who will return the *Web of Life* to its full power, and open the tonal cord energies of the planet, for they are only 12 in number. Only one holds the Master Key, which the rest slot into – she is the 13th, and triply blessed.

She is empowering the mineral kingdom, and is programming the crystals hidden deep in the pelvic bowl of Mother Earth. She is activating the vast crystal chambers and the Crystal Pyramid Temples, for their ultimate return to Planet Earth.

She is beautiful and she is blossoming. She is opening her arms wide and holding the whole planet in her arms, cradling them to her ample bosom and awakening all women to their inherent feminine powers, and their beautiful selves.

She is embracing the male and tempering their masculine power, so that the Earth can be healed by the feminine power, and the balance between male and female returned.

She is love!

She is teaching All Creation to sing the songs of their heart and souls.

She is back!

We are standing on the threshold of dramatic changes, not only in our personal lives, but also social, economic, governmental, and earth changes.

We are dealing with new and different energies, which will usher in a paradigm shift in our relating to each other and in our energy exchanges. Most of all, we will be forced to look for new ways of exchanging energies on a fair basis, – sharing resources and assisting one another, and this planet as a whole to heal.

Thus the Bride is ready for union with her Bride-groom – the one she has been waiting and preparing herself for.

She has been initiated into the *Ancient Rites of Womanhood* and has been anointed by the *Divine Mother* herself. She epitomizes womanhood in its true and beautiful empowerment and therefore her symbol is the **serpent** – not a serpent in the literal sense, but rather a symbol, representing the deeper meaning of sacred energies and sexual rites.

In the magnificent moment when a woman truly stands in her own power, she is deeply and profoundly connected to her own heart and soul. She reconnects to her inner core Being, present since time began, when, in an act of sacred union, she was first conceived and then birthed as a soul.

She knows her own soul name, and she *lives* it with everything she has. For she joyfully and exuberantly expresses the *Divine Essence* in all she is and does, knowing that her true beauty comes from deep within.

She is part of the greater Whole, the Divine and Cosmic Heart – and even more so to the *Cosmic Womb*. For she has the profound awareness that she is as connected to the womb of the Divine Mother, as she is to her own womb, and she nurtures this knowing in this most sacred and powerful area. It is here, that she has her innermost sanctuary, that part of her that has always been hers, and where she feels her true identity most strongly.

Her womb and heart center are intimately connected, and when she has empowered herself in all her four bodies, the physical, mental, emotional and spiritual, then she also has energized herself from deep within. She is *at-one* with all that is, for deep down she IS Creation, and the creative force.

She feels intensely, with a beautiful sensitivity, and a joy of life that extends to all beings. It is here that she wishes to create, and bring that creative love, joy and power to the world. She does not have the brashness and harshness of a conquering spirit, but rather a restrained loving strength. She knows how to stand her own ground if need be, and can become as strong as a lioness defending her cub, when necessary.

She is connected to her womb, for she has worked through all her stuck emotions and feelings, and cleansed what no longer served her highest soul good – wanting to fly free and unencumbered to be her powerful self.

She has done her inner work, until she stands naked and stripped to the core. It is here that her true beauty reveals itself, reflecting her greatness and the incredible mystery of what womanhood entails. She is a power-house, who ignites a flame within her sanctuary.

When she is in sync with her roots, she glows with an inner seductiveness that gives her a deep internal radiance.

Standing there in her true beauty and power, she awaits the man who will enhance all that she is, knowing she doesn't need a man to fulfill her, for she is already complete from within.

Rather, she is looking for a man, who will honor

her womb, and her deepest core heart. She is seeking the one who she can truly let into the innermost sanctuaries, her powerhouse, so that she can open any unexplored parts of her sacred self.

For she can only truly love with her heart open, filled with **trust**, trusting that he can delve into the depths of her being; not betraying or invading her, *but joyfully merging with her as one!*

When he thrusts with the immense beauty, magnificence and splendor of his true heartfelt manhood, she gathers him around and within her, yet opening more and more, until there is just the merging of Love energies, with intense moments of joyful releasing, gathered up and filled to the brim. Then tears of joyful bliss flow, as she finds herself reflected in him and he in her....

The power of a sacred union is unleashed, and vortex energies rise in an act of immense significance, as they lose themselves in the sacredness of the Divine sanctuary. They merge and fuse into that ultimate state, where there is nothing *but ONE single Flame of existence, which becomes the three-fold flame of the Divine.*

When she does discover him, her *divine other,* and there is that deep honoring, she forgets all that she has ever been before. She joyfully welcomes him in – his body, his mind, his emotions, his spirit, but more than this, the very vibration and unique energy of him.

For she understands that this Bridegroom, stands within his own sacred core, and his sacred energy is what completes her.

Such is the holiness of this union – when truth

stands in truth, and love stands in love, and there is no space or breath in between.......

It transforms into the most powerful life changing force – able to create life itself.

To my Beloved
You are to me the Cosmos
the Universal Mind
the Alpha and Omega
that moves with infinite Wisdom
and spans all time and space
And if I look back to that first Creation
when you and I were born
You fit in perfectly with me
in balance, harmony
for love has been there
since that birth
in the oceans of Eternity
And Love will be that carrying force
and ever expanding energy
the swirling twirling infinite Source
the very cells within the cells
the living love
within the love
the music of the spheres
And as we are galactic
we become eternally
for love

is ever rebirthed

within the flames

ignited:

Two mighty

Rivers of Life

the Sun and Moon

flow into ONE

the Tree of Life

arises

ignited

for the

Son/Daughter of Man/Woman...

LOVE IS THE ETERNAL SPIRAL

WITHIN/WITHOUT

ABOVE/BELOW

COSMIC LOVE IGNITED!

LOVE

AD INFINITUM!

LOVE

AD INFINITUM!

LOVE

AD INFINITUM

Judith Küsel

Chapter 12

SHE

She is no longer begging to be loved with all of her being, for she understands that her soul is infinitely connected with All-that-is.

She feels deeply and profoundly, for she is a heart-centered being, who creates with great love, and all those whose lives she touches can drink from the eternal fountain, and find the love that is expressed in trillions of ways.

She loves what she does, and she does what she loves, and is not waiting any longer for the approval of others, for she knows she is unique and special, and needs to live out who she really is – truthfully from her heart and soul. Whether other people understand this or not, is none of her business – her mission is to live her life as best she can, with all that she is, and aspires to be. The rest she leaves in much Higher Hands.

She embraces abundance in all its forms, and she knows there is more than enough for all. She applies the law of giving and receiving equally, and counts her blessings every single day, blessing all whom she encounters, and all the Earth and Heavens.

She is not afraid of being *other-worldly,* for she always knew this planet was not her home, and that she belongs between the galaxies and stars, in infinite abodes, where Earthlings have long forgotten they dwelt.

She converses with the Angels, Archangels and so many beings of the unseen worlds, for she knows they exist just as the denser physical realms exist, and are just as real. She knows this deep in her heart and soul, in those times when she sheds quiet tears from her inner heart in her own space, which no one has ever seen. There were times when she felt the depths of despair and called out in the long, dark nights of her soul, when she had nowhere to go to, nobody to confide in, or share this with. In these moments God, the Archangels, and her guardian angels and higher guides came to assist her, and she will always remember this. Now she asks them every single day to be with her and to guide her every step of the way.

She knows things which others will never know or understand, and she trusts her inner knowing, her inner seeing, hearing and intuition, for it is always right. She has long since learnt that when she ignored it; she would get into trouble. Now she just trusts what is given, even if she sometimes cannot see the bigger picture yet.

She knows things, and has that insight and vision, the wisdom of All Ages deep within herself, and she just loves delving ever further into the mystical, the magical and infinite wonder of life, and that which is beyond the earthly plane. She wants to know the inner workings of all that is, and what lies beyond. She is not afraid to explore beyond the ordinary, and then to trust that whatever is given her, is the truth, for she searches for her own soul truth, and what rings true to her.

She has started loving herself, for all that she is, and she is learning to love every curve, every sinew, muscle, wrinkle and cell, for she is finally realizing the gift of the *sacred temple* that is God/Goddess given, and she is grateful for All of it. She puts time aside to pamper herself, inside and out, and she is not afraid to allow herself *me-time,* time to just be!

She feels vibrantly alive, and filled with the gift of life, and she stops looking at propaganda, the false hype, and images of what a woman should look like, and be. She stops comparing herself with others and beating herself up, and looks rather deep into her own soul for what is truthful, authentic and real for her, and she honors her body as being beautiful and sacred in its own unique way. For everyone has their own beauty – all are born as unique individuals, and no one is made better than any other – the God/Goddess made them all perfect, whole and complete and nothing is missing!

When men (and women) try to make her fall into the trap of competition with others, then she quietly smiles and goes her own way. She is the Goddess after all, she spans dimensions and outer space with her inner being, and she knows that in all the Cosmos there is enough room for everyone, and nobody has to compete for attention, for their own place under the Central Suns – for God/Goddess created the vast firmaments of the Heavens and even beyond all this, and her soul knows no competition there, since everything slots in perfectly, just as it should.

She is very aware and discerning now about her own sacred space, her womb, her most beautiful and treasured womanhood, as a sacred gift to herself and to love. She loves herself, nurtures herself, and does the inner healing work, releasing all the negative emotional cords, hooks and ties. She asks Archangel Michael to cut all of these, freeing herself of all the emotional baggage, and refusing to drag the past, all the past lives, and the ancestral baggage with her any longer. She is learning to fly, unencumbered and free!

She knows that she loves deeply – when she loves she gives it her all, because she can do and be no other, but she refuses to allow anyone to use her as a doormat, or to treat her as a second class, or even as a soulless being, for she has learnt that boundaries are healthy, and she has mastered the fine art of self-respect, self-worth and self-love.

She now honors her own soul – her inner soul radiance, and her most sacred space, thus she is very fussy and discerning about whom she allows into this holy space. She no longer begs for crumbs, she refuses to change and lose herself for any man, or to allow anyone into her energy fields who is not on the same wavelength and frequency as her. She has finally realized she is capable of walking her path alone, in her own strength, rather than allowing herself to become disempowered, or to give her power away to someone who does not see her inner beauty. She is willing to stand naked and vulnerable to the core, with her heart and soul open and nowhere to hide. If he cannot open himself in the same manner, then there will be an imbalance, and she at last understands, the where one is too much, and the other too little, such an imbalance cause pain.

It is not that she is unwilling to be in a relationship, it is just that she finally understands the fullness of her womanhood and the power of her Goddess hood.

She has been through the mill, and been grounded into the finest of dust, been reassembled and reinvented, until she understood that her power lay in her authenticity, truthfulness, faith, inner strength, inner beauty, loving heart, as well as her ability to ride out the storms, and still emerge in one piece. There has never been a time when she was without a roof over her head, a bed to sleep in, and food on the table, for she has been carried on the wings of the angels, and she knows for sure, that she is never ever abandoned or alone.

Now she claims her full Goddess hood – all that she is, she no longer shrinks away from the power of womanhood, but she embraces it all. She stands there fearless, and stands firmly rooted in both Mother Earth and the Divine Cosmos, all that is, and ever will be, and she does not need to be validated for who she is! **She is all!**

Therefore, she will love fiercely, loyally, with her whole heart, mind, soul, spirit, body and being, the man who is fearless in loving her too.

The man who is willing to love her totally, completely, and not shrink away from her power, but stand fully in his own manhood and power too.

She does not want a half-man, or an unconscious man, she wants him to be fully conscious and present with her, whether he understands her or not.

Love doesn't need to be understood, but is best felt and lived every moment with every single breath, and beyond into the mystical realm, where one has to chart new paths, and to open new "true love" ways of relating and being.

When she stands in the fullness and glory of her own womanhood – open, vulnerable, authentic, real, honest, and in her higher soul love, and he likewise stands in the full glory of his manhood, with vulnerability, authenticity, integrity and honesty. Then they both express their innermost soul identity, without masks, and in the magnificence of their soul beauty, they can finally meet as equals, as partners, in balance, and create something extraordinary together.

Eventually they are able to understand that they are not in competition with each other, they are not at war, they are not pulling each other in different directions, nor causing each other pain, but they are actually realizing that their soul calling and purpose is greater than anything else. Then, when they find each other on so many levels, they are destined to work together in tandem, in partnership, going outwards in the same direction, sharing the same vision to raise consciousness, and to work towards the greater good of all.

At last there is the freedom to create new and greater levels of love in relationships, without one being overwhelmed by the other, but each one equally empowered and in love. Walking in love, talking in love, partnering in love. This does not mean that there will not be fireworks, thunder and lightning, and times when the storms come – rather both are mature enough, to ride out the storms; to truly harness that inner soul strength and to find that in the end, everything that has happened has brought them even closer together, to finally understand the immense gift of **true love.**

She has finally come home to a deep resting place, inside herself. She may have lost a lot in the process, her work, her home, her family, her friends. The old life has disintegrated at the very core. Yet, she has found a deep inner belonging, a deep inner peace, a deep love, which spans all dimensions and forms.

She is realizing that happiness is something inside herself, and she no longer looks for it outside. She knows that she is whole and complete, and therefore there is no neediness to find another to fill the void – for the void is no longer there.

Now she can love with a love deeper and more profound, for it is soul love. And she can be all she wishes to be and more!

She is learning to fly high like an eagle and to soar even higher into the galactic and cosmic spaces. She knows no bounds!

Then one day, he comes, her eagle, her mate. They fly and soar and do the mating dance, and she finds they are equally matched. Then, she flies high above him, and she closes her wings and free-falls: – and he catches her with his wings, as she has trusted him to do. Then they reverse the process, and he free-falls and she catches him with her wings.

In total trust, respect, and with a deep honoring of

the soul in each other, they now mate on higher and greater levels than ever before: not because of all the scars, the dark nights of the soul, but rather in spite of them all, and because those battle scars were hard won, and served their souls in immense ways. They are finally able to love on a much more profound level, experiencing the transcendental, Universal love, of the *Divine Male* and the *Divine Female*, and ultimately the true state of bliss.

Then, one day, as she stands there on a high mountain, and thanks Mother Earth for giving her life, for giving her this body for an eyewink in eternity, in order to experience life on Planet Earth. She thanks the Goddess for teaching her to stand in her own power, for reveling and dancing in her own beautiful and profound womanhood, and for giving her the opportunity to finally understand the immense gift of life in this form.

As she raises her hands to the heavens and lifts her face to the sun, waves and waves of love energy run through her and radiate out into the cosmic whole.

She has finally come home!

She.

All-that-is.

ONE.

SACRED SEXUALITY

Chapter 13

How to harness the New Energies

I have been asked "How does one harness the New Energies?"

I simply smile, for a process of awakening takes place, at the exact time that you acknowledge that these energies are there, and you open yourself to start assimilating them. When you work with them, you radiate out like a transmitter (or like a satellite beam sending out the signals from where it is orbiting, so that you can switch on a TV and then tune into the station and program that you want to watch).

First of all it is important to understand that we have a *Divine blueprint*, which looks rather like a geometrical structure or form. This is programmed like a computer chip, and essentially reflects who you are at soul level.

You cannot change that blueprint, but you can work within its framework.

These higher energies work with this blueprint, and start activating the different geometrical patterns within it, which look like a kaleidoscope lit up from within, as every single crystalline form in it is activated, and begin emitting their own color rays.

The Archangel in charge of this whole process is *Archangel Raziel* and he is assisted by *Archangels Metatron and Sandalphon. Raziel's name* means "*Secret of God*" – he is placed near to the Divine Source and hears the Divine conversations about cosmic secrets and mysteries.

When you start learning to anchor in these *Higher Frequency Rays*, you begin to activate the crystalline forms within your physical body that match your Divine blueprint, and so a unique geometrical pattern starts forming around you, composed of minute crystal particles. These form a crystalline body – this is your *Light Body*!

So how do you start assimilating and then harnessing the *Higher Cosmic Frequency Rays* into your physical body and auric field?

The first thing you have to do is activate the *12 Chakras or Energy Systems*[8] within your own body. It is important to note here that you have five of these energy wheels outside your physical body: the *Earth Star, Crown, Causal, Soul Star and Stellar Gateway*. These need to be activated, as the 7 Chakra System cannot assimilate, hold or transmit the higher frequency energies!

The *Stellar Gateway* is approximately 12 inches (30cms) above the top of your head. Its color is Gold. It vibrates at the 6th dimension. *Archangel Metatron* and

---

[8] References to chakra system from Dianne Cooper, Angels and Ascension Teachers Training Course of whom Judith Küsel is a trained teacher.

Seraphim Seraphina are associated with this chakra, and a *Calcite crystal* aids its development. During the *Golden Age in Atlantis,* this chakra was open in everyone, and enabled people to access Source. As the ego started to increase, this center started to close down.

The Divine Source is beaming down higher vibrational energies to the Earth now, to assist in the reconnection of this center. Once fully re-activated, we will be able to comprehend our oneness with spirit. However in order to re-connect, we must detach from our ego and personality self. Very few people have currently activated the *Stellar Gateway*, mainly those who have led secluded highly spiritual lives, but this is changing now. Trying to access the *Stellar Gateway* with the use of hallucinogenic drugs can result in damage such as schizophrenia and manic depression.

The *Soul Star is* located approximately 6 inches (15cms) above the top of our heads. Its color is Magenta. It vibrates at the 5th dimension. The Archangels associated with it are *Archangels Mariel* and *Archangel Zadkiel.* A *Selenite* crystal aids its development.

The Soul Star is the link between the *Stellar Gateway*, the *Causal* and the *Crown Chakra.* It takes the pure energy of the *Stellar Gateway,* and filters it to a level that is appropriate for our current spiritual development.

This is where our soul begins to learn about its oneness with all things, and only through knowing this can it progress onto other levels. At incarnation and death, the soul passes through the Soul Star and reconnects to Oneness.

The *Soul Star* is our 11th chakra. The number 11, a Master number, signifies a new start. It represents the potential we have to reinvent our lives, bringing back the pure spirituality of *Golden Atlantis.*

In Atlantean times, people had a different skull structure. The head was elongated so that the *Soul Star* resided within the skull. Now this center is outside our physical bodies.

To open the *Soul Star,* we must neutralize any mental pollution. Discordant thoughts and beliefs (including those of our ancestors) have crystallized within us and need to be cleared away, before this center can be activated and utilized. Other things which pollute the *Soul Star* include drugs, alcohol, depression and lower astral travel.

When the Soul Star is activated you will experience a profound connection with all things.

The *Stellar Gateway* and the Soul Star together, enable a merging of spiritual and earth energies. The *Stellar Gateway* allows pure Divine essence through from above, while the Soul Star draws up the kundalini and the animal instincts from the earth. These energies blend to become what we know as higher consciousness – our God selves!

The Causal chakra is located 3 to 4 inches (10cms) behind the center of the back of the head. Its color is White. It vibrates at the 4th dimension. The Archangel associated with it is *Cristiel,* and a blue *Kyanite crystal* aids its development.

Through this chakra we receive messages, inspiration and information from the Higher Spiritual Realms.

To facilitate this we need to be able to detach ourselves from our learned beliefs. Meditation and exercises, which still the mind, can assist in the activation of this center.

Once information comes into this chakra, it is sent down into the lower energy centers for distribution throughout the whole body.

Like the Soul star the *Causal Chakra* was also situated within the Atlantean skull structure. Today it is located just outside the skull.

Crown Chakra

This Chakra opens you up to accept light from the soul. Where we become "I AM THAT I AM". The Archangel associated with this chakra is *Archangel Jophiel*.

Earth Star Chakra: Located 6 inches (15cms) below the feet. Its color is black. The Archangels associated with this chakra are Archangels *Roquiel* or Archangel *Sandalphon*. Haematite or black Tourmaline Crystals aid in its development.

The *Earth Star,* and the two chakras in the soles of our feet form a downward pointing triangle which channels Divine Energy through the physical body and into the ground, thereby creating our Oneness with the Earth.

We must activate the *Earth Star* if we wish to develop our Causal, Soul Star and *Stellar Gateway*. The higher frequency link between the upper triangle, and the one from our feet to the Earth Star allow us to renew the energy of the Earth.

When the *Earth Star* functions at full capacity, the

integration of spirit into matter will once again take place. This will aid the healing of Humanity and the planet.

In order for us to truly anchor in the higher frequency rays, all 12 Chakras or energy centers have to be fully activated.

At the same time we must consciously activate the *Mahatma energy* into our cells and our DNA, so that our DNA can be transformed into the same high frequencies, as our chakras spin!

Note here: *In the Northern Hemisphere the wheels of chakras spin clockwise and in the Southern Hemisphere anti-clockwise.*

We also have to regularly cleanse and strengthen the chakras.

The activation of the 12 Chakras thus starts the true vibration of your Soul blueprint, and this in turn then is your highest frequency crystalline form that you then live in, by and through, in your ascended form.

We are at a new evolutionary stage unfolding upon this planet and the status quo is about to undergo an abrupt change. Some of us have been prepared to do this work, for a long time. We volunteered to incarnate upon this planet, at this time, to do this specific work, and with the activation of the new energies we can go full steam ahead facilitating great cosmic and heavenly shifts, reflected here on Earth.

Chapter 14

Male and Female roles in the Consciousness Shift

We are now feeling an immense shift of consciousness as the Earth's ancient centers are reactivated and being transformed into mass energy vortex fields. This will affect everyone to their core as we travel toward a gigantic Tsunami-like wave and move into the higher 5th dimensional state. It is now manifesting faster and faster into a concrete form. Those needing to work through old karmic negative patterns and emotions will feel the effects in a significant way. In order to evolve to higher states of being, old patterns need to be re-created and re-formed to recreate new patterns and leave the chaos behind.

Men will have to re-think what true power really is in order to move into a higher position of aligning themselves with what being masculine really is. The *masculine ideal seems to revel in* power and power play. However, power as with any energy in whatever form can be used for the greater good of the whole, or for the self-servicing control of others.

A true warrior knows how to use his power and

sexuality in an uplifting manner for the greatest good. He does not make war but brings higher wisdom into the equation and dissolves conflict by using this power in the correct manner. He first needs to conquer himself by dying to the old, for it is essential he learns that true power and wisdom come only from within.

This shift will bring him back to love for himself and all humanity with the innate knowledge that power must be tempered with love. Brute force only attracts more brute force. A pliable medium like water finds its way in and around obstacles and sometimes even moves right through them, without needing to compromise its power. Whatever commanding forces are now at play either in business, politics, war mongering or in relationships, they will now start disintegrating.

Women will grow more *womanlike* as in *Goddess* like. They were never meant to become like men and should rediscover all their powers, never allowing them to be taken away again. This is an immense shift, for women have always been the transmitters of the higher energies, as shown in the very different roles of the High Priestess and Priest.

They will return to the *heart space*, and back into a *feeling womb*. They should not allow anyone into that sacred space who is unworthy of being there. With worthiness, I simply mean – of the same frequency and vibration and therefore **Energy**.

When women reclaim their intuitive and loving powers and shift into their true state, they will reclaim the sacredness of their womb and inner being, as they will finally have unlocked the codes and keys enabling them to restore this balance. When both male and female aspects are in perfect balance, there will be equilibrium and that higher state of consciousness. There lies harmony. There lies peace.

Without balance in the cosmos, the firmaments of the heavens would fall apart. This is the greatest lesson or initiations which we as a collective now have to master. Initiation rites were always in actual fact cleansing rites. They purified or cleansed the body, mind, spirit and soul, as well as the auric fields, energy fields and vibrational frequencies. It was considered necessary to experience all these trials, in order to be considered mature enough to become a high priest or priestess. This was not an easy route to consider and required a more highly evolved being, in order to be considered eligible for such an important responsibility of Higher Service!

With the initiation rites came the purification rites. Before allowed entry into the inner Temple sanctuaries in which you served, you cleansed yourself daily, with additional purification processes before having access to the holiest shrines.

Why? During the course of your day in a temple, you contacted many people of lower vibrations than yourself. Some people and places would have had negative energy and during any regular day, you ayhave encountered many vibrational frequencies which tend to attach themselves to your aura and energy fields.

This aspect also relates to maintaining balanced sexual energies. There is an aspect of the sexual act that very few but the Ancients understood. Each time someone enters your sexual energy field, you are allowing them to tap into your life force that stems from the Divine Mother and Father. If you are unaligned with your sexual partner, one could steal energy from the other, or feed off each other's sexual energies. It is worthy to note that some women have partners who may try to hook energy into their pelvic area and that hook remains. The woman then becomes attached to the partner either knowingly or unknowingly and so this allows her partner to tap in her whenever he wishes. If this is not cleared and the hooks removed, she could feel depleted energetically, depressed for no rhyme or reason and could suffer from body problems in the pelvic area causing illness.

One's vibrational field must be perfectly synchronised with your sexual partner and heart feelings of love, mutual respect and tenderness must be shared and soul vibrations balanced. If this does not occur, imbalance arises and the one partner may steal the others energy without even consciously being aware of it. This applies to both men and women.

I often sit back and watch the interplay when a couple is together. I can immediately read who is depleting the sexual energy field of whom. There are huge, ugly hooks visible in the sexual area and sometimes these become slimy black tentacles, which can grow quite large in size. These hooks, if not dealt with and removed, can be carried over into other lifetimes with the result that the couple will do the same thing over and over again and with the same results!

When I do Soul Readings, I will see the soul of the person as the *double helix flame* with multiple coloured strands of light, forming a distinct pattern. What I then see is the muck or debris in certain areas as well as soul and emotional scars which have not been cleansed or healed. All of this pulls their vibrational frequency down.

When we start consciously working with the soul and start clearing the blocks, then the flame starts burning brighter and brighter as it goes up in octaves of frequency until it is totally in line with the collective soul vibration.

This is essentially why one has to clean and purify. This is now going to come to fore more and more, as we move from the old world and its patterns into the new.

When life brings us
the moments
Of constant ebb and flow
Let us remember
That even love
Has its endless cycles
Of moving nearer
And then away...
For love's greatest passion
Will become an all–consuming flame
When not those moments
Of rekindling

In certain quietude…..
Yet, precious then
When we look back
And see how love has grown…
For ever closer we have moved
Despite the ebb and flow…

Judith Küsel

Chapter 15

Sexual Energy

Sexual energy is a force all on its own, and is perhaps the strongest motivating force we possess, but we have long forgotten its true and sacred purpose, and this energy can consequently, be one of the most misunderstood and misused.

When love is completely absent, then the sexual act becomes totally devoid of the ideal it was created for, and it becomes self-serving, which ultimately leads to the feeling of an immense void, for no matter how many partners or sex you have, if you do it simply for self-gratification, then it becomes a dominant ruling force, and like all power eventually becomes self-destructive.

Yet, when two souls truly meet in true union, in which love is the ultimate motivating force, this will develop into a loving, harmonious and transcendental experience.

Note the vast difference between serving only self, and serving the extended cosmic whole! The reality is that the issues concerning the purpose of love and true union, have become very confused.

Many of us seek validation through love and relationships, as we lack a sense of completeness, rather feeling unworthy and invisible in our relationships. Others may feel bad when not in a relationship, believing they are incomplete alone.

In actual fact no one else can give you a sense of self-worth. You are worthy just the way you are! There are no "mistakes" or unworthy souls created, but only greatly loved souls conceived in perfect harmony from sacred Divine union.

There are many different types of partnerships and levels of intimacy, and I am writing this in the context of questions I am asked about soul mates and twin flames.

I have touched on the subject of *Soul Groups* before, and that each *Soul Group* contains 144, 000 souls. Thus within one soul group there are 72, 000 male and 72, 000 female souls and **one** of these would be your other half, or *Twin Flame*.

There is one important thing though to note about *Twin Flames*, however – they rarely incarnate at the same time. Usually one assists from the other side, as a higher guide to the embodied twin flame, since the *Twin Flames* dance can be very challenging. The *ultimate balance* is reflected in the other as a perfect mirror, which brings to light the shadow side of things very clearly.

In some instances, in certain soul groups, like the *Illumined Ones*, the flames between the twins are of such potency, that when there is an imbalance, they will spark off each other, until they re-learn to merge their flame, which releases hugely powerful energies. Souls may have incarnated this time around as a pair, because of their ability to heal the Planet's energy centres, while other twins have other specialized work to do and complete on Earth at this time.

If you think about all the lifetimes that you did not incarnate with your twin, then you will understand, that within your own soul group alone, you had about 71 999, other male souls to choose from if female, and vice versa!

So, during all those incarnations, you may have linked up with a Soul mate love, who was on the same life path as you because of your shared *Soul Group* name, and you would have loved each other and formed a strong bond, for the minute one has a sexual relationship with someone, a bonding does occur, not only physically, but spiritually, mentally and emotionally.

Now, your soul group members are not the only ones you linked up with, some connected up with souls from other soul groups, sometimes with great trauma occurring.

Once one is intimate with anyone, then cords are being formed, which must be severed or cut, otherwise, as in the case of traumatic karma, you will repeat the same old patterns over lifetimes.

So what happens, through the law of attraction, is you will attract those souls you had sex with in other lifetimes again in this lifetime, especially if there are repeating patterns, or karmic and sexual cords attached. There are also cords attached to every single vow you ever made over lifetimes, and Angels who are assigned to enforce those vows.

In this lifetime alone, you will meet up with many soul mates, and those you have karmic links with. Meeting them will always trigger something in your sub-conscious, as soul recognition occurs. Yet, at this time, there is the urgent challenge to heal past life traumas and patterns that pulled you down, so that you can step into a higher way of relating!

What generally happens is that we have the free choice to carry on the old patterns, or to truly look with our soul eyes, understand that these patterns are no longer serving us, and then to cut the cords.

Or, we can meet up with our soul mates, feel the instant bonding, and simply try to cling onto the old familiar pattern, because we fear the unknown.

Others may be unhappy in their relationships, and are looking over their shoulders to see if someone else is going to appear, who will make them happier or more content... That may create further complications...

When there is honor and loving trust in relationship, and a deep respect for your partner, this energy assumes a profoundly sacred form and expression. It becomes an extraordinary power, which can allow us to span dimensions and move into the state of utter bliss, euphoria and total Oneness.

With the return of the *Divine Feminine*, comes the return of sacred sexuality, as symbolized in ancient times by the **serpent**.

However this goes beyond the kundalini energy,

and into the sublime energy of the three-fold flames or three-fold serpents, sometimes depicted as the winged serpent on a staff, or rod.

This form of sexual energy, is the greatest creative power or force that we have ever received, but which was withdrawn by the Goddess, when men sought to control women through this means, and started misusing it for their own self-gratification.

Great achievements in all areas of life are possible when we learn to control and direct the sexual energy towards not only sacred union, but sacred **combined higher service**, where both partners dedicate their lives, to use this energy to raise consciousness, and for the growth and evolution of Humanity.

It becomes a force which can have a tremendous ripple effect on the whole.

Sacred sexuality is therefore a conscious merging of two souls. This might be physical or spiritual, but mostly is a combination of both, and can even take on a purely soul energy form.

It is a communion with the Divine. It is a way of honoring the Divine expression in each other. It has at its core the cosmic law: *As Within – So Without.*

Reflected through the other, you both come face to face with the Source Energy of all Creation, the Source Energy of all there is, and shall be forever more!

It therefore transcends the ego – if becomes a state of Infinite Consciousness merging with Infinite Consciousness in its most creative energy form. This is true union, with much loving, tender and heartfelt love, which honors the beauty of the soul in the other, and find itself reflected in every single cell, sinew and vibration of the physical form, the auric field of the body, and most of all the union of true minds and spirits...

We cannot have this level of union with just any-one. Therein lies the secret. It is important to start honoring the sacredness of your soul and your sexuali-ty, before you can begin to truly understand this. Once understanding dawns, you will seek only this ultimate union, which is the most blessed and sanctified partnership there can be.

We have lost respect for the immensity of our own souls and the powerful energies of our own *being,* with the result that we also cannot appreciate the true soul identities of those we seek union with. Once our hearts change from the very core of our being, we start transforming totally, and are exposed to the naked core to our true soul essence. We are thus able to find the soul who most reflects the same vibrational state of being. Then, and only then, can sacred union occur, for there has to be a profound respecting and honour-ing of self and the other, at a deep soul level, before true union can come.

When love is totally absent, then the sexual act becomes a matter of self-absorption, which ultimately leads to an immense feeling of the void – for no matter how many partners you have or how much sex you have – if you do it simply for gratifying self, then it becomes something which rules you and takes hold of you – like ALL power, and eventually this becomes self-destructive and a method to destroy....

Yet, when two souls truly meet in union, where

LOVE is the ultimate reason for coming together, then this extends into mind, body, soul and spirit, and leads to transcendental union, and to the ultimate experience of the beautiful energy and power of sexual oneness.

The fact is that Humanity has somehow started to confuse the issues around love and most of all started to forget what TRUE UNION is, and what it was ultimately created for. True union brings profound extraordinary love, with sublime bliss beyond that which can be experienced in any other way or form!

Will you be there?

When I just need a hand to guide me

Will you be there when I need a hand to hold
onto to?

When I get confused and lost in a world I
sometimes don't understand and which does
not understand me?

Will you sometimes put your arms around me
and just simply hold me,

Close to your heart?

And let me rest my head

On your shoulders

Until the storms of life depart?

Will you sometimes whisper?

Into my ear:

"You're okay, you're doing fine!

I love you just the way you are!"

Will you be there when the nights are long and
full of shadows?
And when the storms of life break loose?
Will you be there when we share the moment's
laughter and sheer
Joy of living?
Will you be a guardian of this world?
So that AS-ONE we are mystical
Teachers who transform the world?
Will you stay true to the call of your own
Heart
Not being swayed by whatever and whoever
tries to change your mind
And will you allow me to do the same?

Together we can change the world and the
Universe at large,
For in oneness we stand taller than the tallest
tree
And we cast our light over the whole Universe

Such is the power of our love
That it has been since time immemorial
When first we were created as the Divine
Spark –
We were one Ray of Light
And when we split
We became the yin and yang
The male and female

The polarities
That always make us one
But also makes us different
Each one unique
Yet – as One!

We always incarnate together
When there is a great need for
Enlightenment in planets attached to
Universes and galaxies in the far reaches of
Creation….
It is in moments such as these that
We are reunited
And when we look into each other's
eyes,
We see ourselves reflected there.
We see the completeness of our souls
When they dance the cosmic dance
Together
And flow to the sound to the eternal
Music
That brings out the innate harmony and balance
That has always been there
Since time immemorial…..

We do not need mere words to communicate
What is innate in our souls,
We know each other's thoughts

And distance has no meaning
As we are never apart....

I always dreamt of the one who would be all
Who would be at one, Body, Mind, Spirit,
Soul,
Little knowing that we would be brought
together
When both of us had walked different
Paths
Yet these paths ultimately matured us
So that when we met we would be able
To enhance and help each other to truly shine
our Light into this world.

You were my teacher and lover in my past lives
And now we step into the eternal dance
Once again
Ever we are bound by the quest for wisdom
For we are the custodians of information,
wisdom, love,
And we are here to open people's minds to find
their own innate truths.

Ours has never been the road that is wide and
most trodden....
We can never be part of the masses just as the
masses can never be part of us
We stand in ONENESS, – we are all and all are

us
Yet our innate and eternal calling will always set
us apart as we are the teachers and guides
We can be the way-showers but
Never be allowed to lose ourselves
and our Highest Calling to Service in the
process.

We walk lightly on this Planet
for we are eternal Cosmic Beings and this is not
our home....
We see with the eternal vision of the
visionaries,
For we see with the eyes of the soul which is
forever linked to the
Soul-force that created us,
Brought us into Beingness
And whose true children we are....

We have both been through much pain in our
lives
And this gives us the depth of understanding
that we need to extend loving hearts and hands
to others
This is what will lead us to illuminate the world
And lead it into its Golden Age...
For we are the "Shining/Illuminated Ones"
who have been since the beginning of time and
will be forever....

We are like the sun…
We light up the whole Creation
Because of who we are
We are sparks of Light
We are immortal
And for one moment
Are here in Higher Service
Until we resume our
True soul-self once more….

Heart-of-my-heart
Soul-of-my-soul
Spirit-of-my-spirit
Body-of-my-body
A million lifetimes ago
We loved and were love
And we will be so
For love like ours is immortal
And has been for all eternity.

It is to the cosmic tune
We unite as one
It is to the eternal truth
We bow
It is to the wisdom of the ages
That we pay homage
It is to the art of Beingness that
We forever form and re-form

As we bring all into balance
And perfect harmony once more.

As oneness stands together
We are that
As love is immortal
We love
As Light shines
We shine
And as we breathe
The Whole breathes
We are all
And all is us
This is the blessing of our
Fusing together as one.
For as the polarities within us merge in those
moments of forgetfulness
When sheer ecstasy brings us into higher planes
of consciousness
The power of our union releases such
tremendous cosmic power
That we literally light up
And anchor in the Highest Frequencies,
Vibrations and Rays
Of tremendous Divine Consciousness
Into this planet.
Ours is the power to activate the Divine Matrix
And to repair and renew the crystalline grid

around this planet
And to usher in the Golden Age....
Whatever we create together in moments of
sacred union stands forever....
For we are the mirrors and reflection, the very
life-breath of the Divine Source: the masculine
and feminine, the yin and yang
And negative and positive
And in that moment when we
Bring into perfection of union
The two polarities
We release tremendous creative energies into
this planet
And the whole Universe.

Thus we are gods,
You are the sun
And I am the moon
And together we fuse
The greater ALL!

I greet the God in you
And you greet the Goddess in me
And it is in this ultimate form
That we are the children of the
Great Divine Sun God
And have been so
Since time immemorial!

I greet the eternal soul in you
The self-same soul that I am
And in this
We greet our true greatness
Our holy power
And our utmost *beingness.*
I love you!

Judith Küsel

Chapter 16

The Highest Pathways of Love and Being Loved

To love and be loved is an infinitely precious gift.

It is the sublime gift of the original coming together in love, harmony and union, with the *Divine Masculine* being in total balanced bliss with the *Divine Feminine*. These are the moments of creative *oneness* which span the Cosmos, bringing wonder and awe.

Man found extreme delight, awe and wonder in his first union with woman, and she likewise felt the wonder and bliss of being filled with his *male-ness*, moving to a greater awareness within, as she returned to him this expansion she had just experienced, which he, as a man could not experience alone.

There is a hidden mystery here, taught in the *Ancient Mystery Schools*, which adds to the Christed consciousness and awareness. If such a union took place, in the purity of Love, it rose into a new state of dimensional expansion, and Higher States of God Awareness were reached by both partners.

For this to occur, they had to be total balanced and harmonized.

A *perfect one,* in union with another *perfect one,* brought about the awe-inspiring expanding gift, of conscious awareness inside and out.

*Such was the gift of those trained in the profound Myster-ies, who knew that unless the inner man and woman were in balanced harmony, they would not be able to manifest this **in the physical realm** through their Divine Union.*

In fact, they taught that to attain the ultimate *En-light-en-ment* one first had to understand the depth of what it meant to be a man or woman spiritually and physically, and only then would such a union be possible. Without doing the inner work, the outer could not manifest into form.

In the *Garden of Eden*, both the man and woman were in a state of innocence. They lived in this union, and knew only ultimate bliss. However they were unable to appreciate it!

The *Fall from Grace*, was in a higher sense, the fall from innocence.

The moment we began separating sexual energy from the very life force, and the Loving state of the highest Soul consciousness within, we felt disconnected from each other, and therefore separate from God.

Since that time, humanity has been seeking whole-ness again, mostly through loving relationships.

However God declared that humans could only return to the *higher states* of Innocence, when they used their woundedness as the means to heal themselves. Once they had been healed, they would find the keys and codes to return them to the original sense of inner unity.

The central key here is wholeness and inner balance, so unless individuals were willing to remedy their wounds and flaws, they were denied access to previous states of blissful innocence. Only when both partners were healed and restored, would they be able to truly bond once again.

Only in this vulnerable state, naked and stripped bare to the core, can we achieve this ultimate state of awareness of the bliss.

In the Ancient *Mystery Schools* individuals were guided through a series of initiations (to do their inner work to regain a state of Innocence) before they could experience ultimate union, in *Divine Partnership* with the *Divine Other*.

This was the true and deep union of two souls, equally whole and balanced, who had been taught to return to wholeness, through merging on all levels, *mind, body, spirit and Soul*.

The physical body became a tool for simultaneously experiencing a heightened awareness of this union of mind, spirit and soul.

In such a union lies the ultimate **En-light-en-ment**, as the *third force* is ignited – the God–Force, the Creative Force, which brings t*he Christedness*, and the Central Sun Consciousness into the state of illumination.

It was no accident that Jesus had Magdalene; Simon the Magus had Helena, and the Pharaoh had his consort, as originally they were the highest initiates of the Mystery School, and were evenly matched. So the *cobra* was the sign of the state of the Enlightenment within, and the true use of the Creative Force, Shiva and Shakti etc., the list goes on and on.

Here two people had a **greater vision, and greater purpose to work towards.**

They looked and walked outwards in the same direction, feeling the profound calling to highest service, in close liaison with each other.

True Love.

True Partnership.

Equal partners.

Walking hand-in-hand, working shoulder-to-shoulder and ever moving towards the greater Creation they were making together.

Thus one was not less than the other.

They were both equally empowered.

*They enhanced each other, bringing out the **Higher Cosmic Consciousness** within each other, and then amplified this through a merging of all their bodies into one single force.*

Two mighty Rivers of Life flowed into each of them, like a double helix strand, and then came the third, the God force as a Lightning Rod, upholding and igniting the two, as they merged into a single energy force.

*Jesus could not have done his work on earth without Mary Magdalene, for she was the force behind his force! They were, in fact the beings created out of the **True Gnosis, True Union**, which had been known to Humankind since the Garden of Eden, but only taught and understood by a very few, trained in the Ancient Mystery Schools of yore.*

This is the highest path of purity, innocence and the ultimate path of En-light-en-ment.

It was something kept secret, for most have worked mainly with their lower animal natures, and lower sexual energies, never attaining the ultimate union, and refusing to do the inner work. Most are just ignorant, believing everything that society has programmed them to believe.

Only the true seekers ever attained these higher states, having strived to do the inner work required.

Here lies an Ancient Hidden Knowledge, and this awareness expands the more you understands the mysteries within.

Let those who have inner eyes, see.

Let those who have inner ears, hear.

Let those who are ready to receive this message, receive it.

So be it.

The inexpressible lies in my heart and soul...

There in between all the nuances
Lie the moments
Crescendoed in a magnitude of waves
When what I feel is immense...
I do not know what to say....
I never expected this....
And it is as if
I want to move into a state
Where I am .... no longer here...
I am Aphrodite... and Venus...
I am ... yet am not...

It is the luscious rising

Of a long forgotten and forbidden ME....

And I love her...

This woman...

Reflected here....

For she is beautiful... powerful... magnificent –
WOW!

And she is set free

To wildly ride the crest of the waves

Exuberant.... deliciously exquisite...

Beautiful...

Bountiful...

ME!

Judith Küsel

Chapter 17

Mystical Marriage – the Ultimate Union

There is a deep and profound union, truly of the body, mind, heart and soul, which is the ultimate alchemical fusion, and transcendental transmutation of the mystical ocean – the *deepest deep* one can experience, in the union between the **Divine Masculine** and the **Divine Feminine**.

When they are both equally empowered and therefore on a par with each other, then the mystical can move in, and the depth of the magical cosmic infinite ocean is there to dive into, explore and to manifest into being and form.

In the *Ancient Mystery Schools* it was understood, that the *Divine Masculine* energy, in its purest form, was a proactive force, which brought action into being, as well as all the cosmic equations, the structure, the movement and the firmaments. Thus the very foundation on which the cosmic order is built, was put in place. It is the *Higher Mind in*fused with the **Higher Heart Mind**, which truly creates the concepts, the formulas, the engineering, the architectural structures, places and positions in the firmaments, in the *Cosmic*

Whole.

The *Divine Feminine* is the *receptive and creative force.* When she stands in her highest empowerment, she creates from her core. She receives the incredible structuring and inventiveness of the *Divine Masculine* into herself, and **creates** all into being. In other words, she is able to manifest into being, what he has envisioned! The cosmic order is formed from his higher heart/mind, and she is the creative force anchoring this, thus creating the metamorphosis. She shape shifts into anything she wishes, for she IS all Creation and Creation is her. Without her, the male cannot complete the Cosmos, he needs her to introduce balance and harmony, and through her the form is created.

More than this, she takes his whole into her, and **energizes** him.

He gives to her, she receives and energizes his gift, then returns it to him in *creative energized form!* Eventually what they have thus co-created, brings new creations into energetic form, and conscious expansion occurs.

Together they fuse into the **Godhead,** as **One,** and in this *oneness,* the ultimate third force emerges, which is sometimes called **The Holy Fire**, or the *Holy Spirit, or Holy God-Soul.* Therefore the true God Energy has both the masculine and feminine equally within it, amplified by the *sacred fire.*

When all components are present, all of Creation moves, for such a union is the mystical union, the ultimate, infinite Source Energy which no-one can define, but which is there, manifesting through myriads of life forms, and also in that which is form-less. It is the primal force which no mind can comprehend. It moves through the soul energies, and into the true union between the heart and mind, and then into the **experience** of this union, which is the mystical essence.

So, in those Mystery Schools the acolytes were carefully screened to find those souls who would be prepared to be dissolved, dismantled, and then reassembled, with the greatest purity of intent throughout the process. They often underwent severe initiations and tests, to gain deeper understanding of this mystical, transcendental process, and so were able to fine tune their inner soul connections, and experience soul empowerment from deep within.

In such experiences the mystical took on new form and meaning, each individual had their own unique experiences, as the mystical is indeed deeper than the deepest depths of *all-that-is*. It was therefore, a continuous quest to delve ever further into this infinite void, or realm, into that which one cannot name, but only experience.

You could only step into the priesthood and then the High Priesthood, if you were prepared to participate in and experience the ultimate Mystical state-of-being. Through the mystical, Source Energy reveals its face in millions of ways, and so you would have to move beyond all veils of illusions, ever deeper into the realms of not-knowing, not-being, the *nothing-state*, in order to dissolve completely, and allow yourself to become reassembled again, in an even greater and higher form.

Very few individuals ever made it to that ultimate state, for they lacked the courage or the total commitment required to walk this path and to embark on this Quest for the Higher Meaning and Purpose of the Grail; truly allowing themselves to be open and vulnerable and ready to experience the mystical in infinite sublime forms.

The Mystical Marriage *was that which was given to those already living with higher insight and understanding, in order for them to truly experience pure love in its ultimate form, and to endure the process of being reborn on multiple levels.*

To do this you have to be prepared to allow the self, the ego, that negative part which always trips us up in some way, with the illusions of fear, of self-service and self-sabotage, to move into the state where you allow the mystery, the ultimate Life-force energy, the Ultimate cosmic energy flow to move through you. You became a *conduit and transmitter* of the Divine Masculine and Feminine Energy, for in this union, you became God and Goddess! Therefore it was considered holy and sanctified, sacred to the very core.

Through increasing the soul energies, calling and purpose, the power and impetus was heightened in turn, so positively affecting the greater whole.

The sacred union was totally dedicated to serving in this manner, in order to *create the Sacred energy force and* energy field, which could then send its ripple effects down the *cosmic matrix* energy fields, (in this case the earth's energy fields), and to the *collective consciousness* energy fields and *super consciousness* energy fields.

The latter was only reached when both partners attained a certain maturity, having demonstrated their total dedication to higher service, but also a true love for the Divine Other, such that the love-bond between them was unbreakable.

For true Mystical Union cannot have more than two within its core, in order to create the third amplifying force.

It was known after the *Fall of humanity*, that very few souls would ever be able to regain this *sacred mystical union*, for most had neither the discipline, nor the desire to delve deeper into mystical union, because they were sidetracked by baser instincts, and a need for instant gratification.

True love is seldom found if you are unwilling to endure discomfort together. Love bonds deepen when experiencing either the deepest shadows or the greatest light, leading to a profound experience of the mystical.

The depths of darkness and despair can only be understood by entering the *Underworld of Hades, then emerging triumphant into the Supremely High Heavenly Light of the Central Cosmic Suns, with their blinding light of Illumination*. Both serve in their own way to hone the inner awareness of the soul, as it experiences the transcendental and the mystical.

It is a hero's journey. For in order to truly experience mystical Love, first of all there has to be balance.

The Masculine Divine must be fully empowered, and likewise the Feminine Divine.

One cannot be too much – and the other too little.

They are equal partners.

They walk hand in hand, shoulder to shoulder, outwards in the same direction.

Their Soul Missions and Purpose is the same.

They are very much alike – but also total opposites. The polarity of opposites is needed in order to engender the Divine Spark and its electrifying effect, thus creating the **balance**.

It is in this paradox that true wisdom is found.

The sacred union works on the same principles and chemical reactions, as those of the rest of the Cosmos, for we were all created from one and the same energy source.

Every time the soul allows itself to go through these highest initiations, it is further enabled to experience true love at a much deeper level. Then the mystical will reveal her transcendental face in a myriad of new experiences and forms.

True love within the sacred mystical union, is always amplified and empowered to radiate forth. It is the ultimate enlightened *state-of-being,* which emerges from such union, and therefore is the highest possible path.

Let those who have the innate understanding, understand this truth, which is proclaimed for them.

She is finally learning to trust again

She is finally learning to trust again
To open her heart and her soul…
To move into her sacred power….

And to treasure the secret sanctuaries
Of her innermost self…
She is learning to open herself
To his magnificent manhood
As he finally learns
That his manhood
Reflects his innermost heart,
The soul of his Being,
That which makes him truly a man….
He gets out of his mind,
And conquers his greatest fear
Of losing control…
She moves past all her fears
Of being conquered
And used
And then discarded at whim….
Something beautiful happens
As finally
All of that fear vanishes
As mists before the sun…
He comes in the splendor of manhood…
She opens herself in the magnificence of her
womanhood…
And two mighty Rivers of Life
Flow and intertwine…
Orgasmic
Serpent like waves

Merging into ONE Being
With two different strands....
As in blissful ecstasy
The I dissolves: –
WE
A third flame
Enshrines the holiness –
Sublime sacredness
Rises
One soul
One flame
One River of Life
The sacred
Tree of Life
Is
Reborn.....
The cosmic cycle
Moves...
Sun
Merges
With
Moon....

Judith Küsel

WHAT ARE
TWIN FLAMES?

Chapter 18

Flame Love: Seeking the Mystical Path for the
Highest Service to the Divine

When the soul was created, it was formed from *12
flames,* to first and foremost reflect a *divine attribute* back
to the Divine. As such the soul experiences certain
characteristics, essences or traits of the Divine in all its
forms and expressions, both the shadow and the light.
By the soul undertaking this, the Divine can then
experience these through its all its Creations.

When time began and the first volunteer settlements lived on the surface of Earth (the *Inner Earth
civilization Agartha,* existed long before the outer crust
of the Earth was formed, as a satellite civilization of the
Intergalactic Fleet), it was felt the *Twin Flames* needed
to uplift and co-create with the Earth's energetic fields
and the cosmic Super-consciousness fields.

There was a specific call for particular *Twin Flames*
from a specific milieu. Most of these souls had been
involved with earth from its very beginnings as
scientists aboard Motherships and they shared a great
love for Earth. They were *volunteers* with *specific* work.

The Ancient Mystery schools were attached to the

first *12 Crystal Pyramid Temples of the 12 Tribal People of the first 12 Tribes* that had developed from these settlements. Each Temple worked on a different *Cosmic ray*, with a different color vibration and frequency, and the inner Temple staff worked with a specific ray performing a specialized task. (Some temples had more than one task to fulfill, but this is covered in my new book: '**Why I was born in Africa.** The previously unrecorded history of Elysium and The Lion Kingdom**.**')

Specific soul groups were involved in this whole venture, e.g. *The Illumined Ones, The Loving Ones, The Graces*, and so on. Those *Twin Flames* from these groups normally have a very high sense of calling from birth, though some just arrive here, extremely focused with a deep and profound sense of destiny. They certainly know they are here to do specific work and so are often very service-orientated. They are drawn to professions where they can help the community at large, perhaps as an engineer, architect, doctor, healer, counselor, librarian, writer, teacher, philanthropist, and so on. They will serve in every way they can and often blaze new trails for humanity.

When the *Twin Flames* of these specific groups meet, there is an instant recognition of the *Divine Other*. They just know. With it comes the deep knowledge that their unions are here to serve a *greater purpose,* and by combining their forces, their own mission will be amplified. With the union and merging of the two flames, they ignite the third and *Greater Flame or Fire*, and so reach an even greater audience, or frame work, and a larger platform than if they worked alone.

It is here that the proverbial chaff is separated from the wheat, for these *Twin Flames* will always share a common m*ystic calling* and it will not just be one of them; it will be *both* of them for they are reflected in each other. They are called to the *Highest Mystical Path* into total dedication to serve the three-fold flame of **Love, Power** and **Wisdom**. Not all fall in this category and those who follow this path will have recognized this long before I recorded this.

These *Twin Flames* have a long history of serving and being initiated into the *Ancient Mystery Schools of Elysium, Lyra (Lion Civilization), Lemuria, Atlantis, Greece, Egypt, Balkans, the Ural Mountains, and Mexico.*

All have within their energy fields certain engraved symbols that identify them and those who read these will immediately know for who and what they are and in what capacity and under which ray they are serving. The higher the rank of these souls, the more these signs will be illumined on their forehead and also under their left breasts and on their upper arms.

A record of this is kept In the Ancient Mystery Schools in the Great White Lodge on Sirius, as well as in the Super-Consciousness Energy field of the Divine. These can never be faked or ever removed. They were earned.

*These souls endured stringent initiations in the inner and outer planes and at the Mystery Schools of the Divine Source and therefore these symbols are easily recognized. It is a subconscious recognition of high initiates and they simply **know**.*

These souls are those who were always drawn to the mystical. No other pathway appeals to them. They can do and become no other than mystics ever delving deeper and deeper into the *Mystical, Gnostic, Tantric, Trinity which is the eternal three-fold flames and those attributes of God which makes it the greatest Mystery of Eternal life and love force.*

For these Twin Flames will then go through intense initiations into that inner seeing, with the opening up of heart energies, through the seven gateways of sexual energy.

This path calls for both to be stripped back to their innermost selves, to become vulnerable and fragile which then allows love to re-form and re-birth them.

This is essentially the highest path of the crucifixion. It is the path where the Old Adam and the Old Eve have to die, in order for the New Adam and Eve to be born. It is in dying that resurrection comes bringing with it the Knowledge of the *Tree of Life* and the opening of the portals to Eternal Life.

In that dying moment, the third force, the eternal Divine life force makes itself felt, as the *force of resurrection.* This is that force from which all life has sprung, the eternal breath, Presence and Mystery, as deep as the deepest cosmic ocean and unfathomable, unknown and eternally creatively present!

It is through that intense moment of union, when one loses oneself completely in orgasmic joy, with the immense release of the serpent energy, hovering between worlds, that one may experience this inexplicable force.

If you are not open to the very heart of all life with

a profound yearning to become At-One with the Mystery, then you cannot expand into this vast energy field where you literally dissolve into nothingness to become the Divine Force, to be reassembled again.

The greater the love is, the greater the flame between the Flames and therefore the ever greater call to Higher Service.

This union is not about **Me.** *It is not about* **Us.** *it is about* **We** *as one heart, one mind, one body, one soul. It is about how we can* **serve** *the greater whole with our union. How can our love for each other, our calling, our purpose and our serving ignite the eternal cosmic flame in the hearts and souls of many? How can our union make a difference to the world?*

See, how everything shifts.

This is what Christ is all about.

It is that intense flame, that eternal quest of the soul to truly serve the Divine in each and every way it can through this Mystical pathway of Sacred Sexual Union.

It is a Path.

It is a Calling.

The minute a soul decides on the Higher Path and reconnects with its Higher Soul Self then the Over-Souls who are the Higher Beings in charge of the overall soul growth, will summon the soul for a briefing to create a Soul Contract.

During this briefing we are shown our history and the soul contract is signed before incarnation. We are shown where we are still on track with that contract, the lessons we wished to master, and a road map for the future.

Sometimes we are on track, but may have been side-lined and distracted along the way. Life here can feel controlled by certain parties who utilize their power to control mass consciousness. We can then get caught up in this illusion and spun around forgetting our own power and innate abilities.

Other times we may go awry and oftentimes something drastic will occur, like a near-death experience to jerk us out of illusions, back onto the right track once more.

Once the soul agrees to return to its Higher Soul Path, it will endure a period of initiation and purification, mainly because certain lower vibrations on earth, may attach themselves to souls.

Sometimes, this inner cleansing and realignment can be a period of intense releasing. The proverbial carpet will be and can be pulled out from under the soul in order to serve its higher growth. Anything that no longer serves enlightenment, will start falling away, whether these events come to us in the form of relationships ending, jobs lost, financial ruin or trauma. Decisions will be necessary and life changes occur with possible pain and feelings of loss or dread. It may feel that layer by layer the outer core is being stripped away systematically until at the inner core, the heart and soul lies bare, exposed and extremely vulnerable.

What is occurring is the dying off of the old and the re-birthing of the new soul. It is a process and yet with each shedding, the soul becomes lighter and brighter. Radiating and shining forth. The master painters used to paint halos around saints' heads, because this is literally what starts happening as the higher chakras, or energy centres in the crown chakras are activated and the **stellar** gateways opened. The soul is then opened up to Higher Communication with the Divine Source.

During this initiation period, we will always be guided, as the right teachers appear and correct guidance steps in.

Fear may be the greatest factor in stemming soul growth. When a soul is clinging onto the old and fears letting go or stepping past the self-seen barriers and into the virtual unknown, we often need to be nudged gently to step past all of that. Then we will be guided towards obtaining the Keys or codes needed to step past that hurdle.

It is so important to keep up and keep working with the heart center and the thousand petal rose of the heart.

Each petal of this rose connects to a certain consciousness energy center in the physical and emotional body, and will then work with the opening of those centers which are blocked, or not functioning at optimum levels.

When the heart center is closed, the lower energy centers and those above the heart center cannot function properly. This is the central hub around which all creation functions. Every single cell in our body also links to this vital center. In that moment the eternal life fire is lit, the **Fire of Illumination**.

That is the supreme gift of the Gods.

Yet, never this to use in self-service, only in highest ser-

vice.

Let those who have ears — hear.

Let those who have eyes — see.

*Let those who have the inner understanding — under-
stand.*

The rest sleep the sleep of forgetfulness.

I think of you

Your image is cast in the heart of my soul
Eternally there
Lifetimes have come
Lifetimes have gone
And as all changes in energy, form...
There was not one moment
When love was not there....
I think of you
And my fingers long to etch its way
Across your face
I think of you
And heart expands
Into the infinity of particles
Which make the cosmic whole....
I think of you
I love you.
Eternally loved you.
Eternally will.

Judith Küsel

Chapter 19

Soul Names, Groups, Mates and Twin Flames

The Divine created all in that first moment when the Great Divine Mother birthed all of Creation from then onwards, because Creation is an ongoing process and every second new souls, new constellations, star systems and planets are being formed. Thus She gave birth to a group of souls.

The first Soul Groups numbered 12 in total. Their creation saw the corresponding birthing of the first 12 color rays emitted by these Soul Groups, a unique frequency and vibration and a particular expression of soul gifts or creative force that the Divine wished to experience in multiple phases. It desired to know what it is to feel and express the specific gifts, traits, talents, abilities, sounds and tones.

The Soul Group expression reflects back to the Divine everything it wishes to experience concerning the life force!

These 12 form the core *Soul Groups* and it is from these that for instance, the *Illumined Ones* stem.

Since then the Divine has created additional groups, there are now younger Soul Groups, yet all were created to express a certain talent, trait, feeling, or thought form that the Divine Source wanted to experience via the souls.

At this moment many souls from the core group of 12 have incarnated, as they originally laid down the Web of Light and helped establish life forms here. They are here specifically to assist with holding the light steady and to help the shift of consciousness and the healing of Earth. *Within their souls and Soul Groups specific codes exist encoded with knowledge that will be increasingly activated so as to be of higher service to humanity to help by ushering in the new Golden Age.*

These are old Souls who have had one or more previous incarnations on earth, most often in Elysium/Avalon, Lemuria, Mu, and Atlantis. Some are highly evolved and were asked to return at this time, while others chose to incarnate with their *Twin Flames* so their combined flames could be used to assist earth's healing.

Each Soul Group consists of 144, 000 Souls and has a *unique name, vibration, frequency, and color and sound traits with its distinctive creative expression.*

Each Soul within a Soul Group has a unique *Soul Name*. This will bear the same vibration, frequency, sound, trait and creative expression, and also a unique gift or gifts or Soul expression of that Soul Group.

For instance there is a Soul Group which has the soul name, **Grace**. The Soul Groups have their own frequency, vibration, color and sound and their Soul expression is to *experience grace, to give out grace and to learn to live through everything connected with grace* – the whispers, nuances, and life experiences associated with the expression of grace. So, a soul in this group could have a name like this: *He or she who has to learn to live in grace and be graceful…..*

Now, look closely. The group is learning to express grace, and to live in grace. Their life here will be a learning to live and give grace in all its various expressions of that. They might find themselves in circumstances where they are challenged to forgive others who hurt them, so that so that through this forgiveness, they can give them grace. They will vibrate via their soul name, on a vibration that emits the same vibrational frequency as the Soul Group, with the same color ray within their own color and the same sound within their soul sound/tonal cord.

They will act as a magnet to all souls incarnated now who vibrate on the same frequency, color, ray and sound!

During this time, souls are being united to work as one so that their innate talents and abilities may be used to hold the light to help heal the planet and raise consciousness. They will attract those on the same frequency band and will emit the same color ray, sound and soul expression, which in this case is, Grace!

Their soul mates will be from the **Grace** Soul Group and their *Twin Flames* (if incarnated) will also be from this group! Moreover their *Twin Flame* will match or enhance the qualities of their own names!

Twin Flames are each a double or multiple flame and when they come together in body, mind, spirit and soul *they become one flame* and emit a very potent energy source or flame!

This does not mean that if you are from one Soul

Group, you cannot love another from a different group. It is just more likely that a *Soul Mate* or *Twin Flame* union will be far more likely to succeed. The combined vibrational frequency of two souls from the same group will be far stronger and more anchored into the *Soul Group's* vibrational frequency. This union will be closer, stronger, more potent, happier and more content, as they are in tune with each other and can make beautiful music together – as one!

I will be concentrating on the *Twin Flames* of the *Illumined Soul Group* who have been involved with earth from the very beginning. The Illumined Soul Group originates mainly from Andromeda, Pegasus, Arcturus, and the Pleiades. This is where the first Soul Cluster Group of the Illumined Ones started to work.

When the Earth was first colonized, the first continent, (remembering that there was only one continent that time) was occupied by inhabitants and scientists from these Galaxies. When this continent first had difficulties with the *Web of Light*, (after an asteroid hit the planet and threw the whole grid out of balance), the Intergalactic Council asked for *Twin Flames* from the *Illumined Soul Group* to volunteer to assist with the whole process of healing the Web.

Thus the first *Twin Flames* from Andromeda and Pegasus arrived, and in a specific ritual which was performed through sexual union, the grid was repaired. (I will only mention this element here) There are many factors involved in this. It is not only the fact that the twins emit such high frequency light, but their union had to take place within a certain environment, with the aid of certain structures and tools. (My books have more details).

In this process the twin became separated from his or her other half, and thus felt incomplete at some deep soul level.

During the course of the history of the Earth, more and more *Twin Flames* incarnated here. However, during the great falls into oblivion that the Earth experienced on numerous occasions (Elysium, Lemuria, Atlantis, etc.) *Twin Flames* were subsequently separated, and so loaded a lot of karma onto themselves. They started to take on distinctive male and female forms in their incarnations, and seemed to repeat the same patterns time and again.

In this process the twin became separated from his or her other half, and thus felt incomplete at some deep soul level.

At this moment in our collective history a few hundred of these *Illumined Twin Flames* have incarnated, for they, more than the other twins, have accumulated a large amount of karma. Their challenge in this life is to find each other again, and then to work towards balance and equilibrium, so that their energies can be reunited, and finally used in the ancient form of union, in order to heal Planet Earth and the Web of Light.

However, and here is the big challenge, these two will really push each other's buttons, and as much as the sexual magnetism between them will pull them together, they will also spark off and trigger each other, in their search to find balance, between the male and female aspects or energies within themselves.

What normally strikes people about these two is how much alike they are… They might look alike and act in ways that mirror each other, and their lives seem to be parallel at some level, e.g. they may both be teachers and writers etc.

Throughout the course of the history of this planet, more and more *Twin Flames* incarnated here. However, during the great falls into oblivion that the Earth experienced on numerous occasions (Elysium, Lemuria, Atlantis, etc.) *Twin Flames* were subsequently separated, and in so doing burdened themselves with substantial karma. They now started to take on distinctive male and female forms in their incarnations, and seemed to repeat the same patterns time and again.

For when the heart is not engaged, with the mind, spirit, soul and body then all relationships are bound to fail in one form or another!

We are stepping into higher states of consciousness and if your awareness level does not match up with that of your partner, you are likely to soar in higher dimensions and your partner will be left dragging their feet in the lower ones.

In Ancient Times when you wished to link up with someone, you went to the Temple of Love, and the High Priestess read your soul records and those of your partner to establish whether your Soul Groups were a match. They ascertained if your vibrational frequencies, sounds and colors matched. When all were perfectly matched, then a blessing was given to the union – for now whatever took place, would be in loving harmony and oneness!

Children were conceived in beautiful harmony and sexual energy was used for higher purposes it was intended for – to connect people with higher states of consciousness and the divine source.

There is nothing random in the universe. We are here because of soul contracts with certain qualities to express. When we combine this with loving soul unions, we start truly stepping into the Higher States of being and learn a totally new way of relating with an open heart and soul, and so a higher way of loving evolves.

Then why Soul Mates or *Twin Flames*?' Mostly because it will be much easier to have a true body, mind and soul relationship with someone from the same Soul Group and is vibrating at the same soul frequency.

When we end up with someone who has a different Soul Tune or frequency, we tend to be out of tune with them. We might be in tune for the first few months and years and then suddenly wonder what happened as we are singing different songs in different chords!

This is ancient knowledge and one that most religious organizations have suppressed as they do not wish people to empower themselves at soul level!

When you know who and what you are at soul level, and you heal at soul level and step into a different octave of consciousness, you have learnt to vibrate in harmony with the Soul Group vibration amplified 144 000 times!

Therein lies the key! Once united with your soul

mate or *Twin Flame*, you immediately begin to amplify the vibrational frequency not double, but multiple times which is the making of bliss. It is here that both twins learn how to handle this potent source of energy, knowledge, wisdom and the truth about sexual energy. When we, re-learn how to relate and how to become truly intimate in soul relationships we will step into a vastly different arena! For some it is already happening and for others this will be happening soon.

This is the time to learn to dance with the cosmic and earth energies, and with the soul mates or *Twin Flames*, incarnated with us at this time, so that we can truly assist earth to ascend, and in the ascension process, collectively, raise the consciousness of others. This is the main reason why we are here!

I treasure my most inner sanctuary

And then found one day
You entered there
For my innermost sanctuary
Is the very core of me
And there I am the
The Goddess of my Realm…
Yet, there you were
And you filled it…
Filled with immense
Potent energy
Which ignited flames

Within

And without

Transforming

The sanctuary

Into the realms

Of the

Gods and Goddesses

Of the

Eternal Gardens of delight…

Where

Reigns

Bliss

Ecstasy

Euphoria

My sanctuary

My treasure

Innermost

Sanctuary

Is

Now a

Temple

A Divine

Temple

Of

Delighting

Love

Love

Expressing
Love
Flames
Of
Love
Igniting
With
The
Central
Sun

Judith Küsel

Chapter 20

The Cosmic Dance of the Twins

The soul is not bound by time and space, but lives eternally. It lives as sheer Light energy, and emits not only light, but sound and colors. It vibrates in harmony with the light frequencies and sound (tonal chord) frequency band of the Soul Group, or Over soul. This in essence is the I AM presence, which is in all of us.

When the soul is fully activated, it has 12 distinct flames, and these flames then form part and parcel of the **13th flame**, which in essence is the flame of the **Holy Spirit**, or the flame of the Over-soul, as embodied in the collective soul group spirit, which in turn forms part of the greater *cosmic flame*, the *threefold flame,* of **Love**, **Power**, and **Wisdom**.

When we incarnate onto a very dense and hostile planet (and it is *not* Mother Earth who makes it so, but those who wish to control this planet for their own hidden agendas), the soul experiences amnesia. As a child we might remember something, but the status quo soon tries to shut down our pineal and pituitary glands, so that we cannot receive *cosmic transmissions* of Light from our Soul Group, the Cosmic Hierarchy and most importantly the Divine.

I am going into some detail here, so that you can understand that you vibrate at a soul frequency (which is hidden in your soul name which is very different from any earthly name, as it epitomizes the frequency band your soul vibrates on.) When this is fully activated, someone not of that frequency band, will fall off the bus, so to speak. For a frequency band will only be able to sustain what is on the same band, and when one tunes into that same frequency, then there is unity and harmony. Anything discordant with that, cannot exist there, it might disrupt the energetic frequency. When fully activated and over-lighted by the collective Soul Group, and the Divine itself, it will automatically revert to its own frequency.

You can think of this like a radio. When you tune into the frequency band of your favorite station, you might find disturbances, until you are at exactly the right frequency, and can hear properly without distortion.

In this lifetime we all search for the ideal love and loving, and dream of ultimate happiness, the unity that we on a soul level, remember as a state of harmony and bliss.

Our soul, in all its 12 flames or parts, has had many lifetimes, in many forms and existences, and not only on this planet. For example, I know that a part of my soul is pure light frequency. It vibrates at such a high frequency band that psychics have often told me that they cannot see form, but only streaks of pure Light. This part of me is attached to the Divine Source, and that is where it works in Temples or Halls of Wisdom, Higher Teaching, Healing and Records. This is one of the reasons that I can tap into the highest and purest soul records. Another part of me is attached to the Andromedan and Galactic Core Federation, and likewise the Pleiadean and Sirius worlds. There are thus different parts of me, working and living simultaneously, with this form I have chosen here on Earth. In reality only a tiny fraction of me has incarnated, the other parts are still working elsewhere in the Cosmic Whole.

In truth I am a Cosmic Being, having a short sojourn here on Earth to complete my mission.

It has taken me a while to understand this concept, and I am often asked about it, and that is why I am sharing this with you, not to boast, but in all humility, so that you might have a greater understanding of the magnificence of your own soul.

The truth of our soul, our soul group and the Divine truths are deliberately withheld from us. Until we start reconnecting with our true selves, and building our Lightbridge back to the Divine, to activate our Stellar Gateways and Soul Star Chakras (which are huge transmitters, and connect us to our own Divinity as held within our soul groups), we cannot be fully activated and empowered.

This planet is in the process of a major revamp, and so is the collective whole. Some souls who have incarnated since World War II are the same beings who were involved here from the beginning; who have returned to hold the Light steady and to anchor in highly advanced knowledge and understanding. They thus are here on a specific mission, and for a very specialized task. I call them the **Illumined Task force**.

Some souls are *volunteer* souls, from other galaxies and star systems, that have never experienced war of any kind – not even the Wars of the Heavens. They came in with immensely powerful technological tools, and higher healing abilities to assist us to move from the third to the fifth dimensional state. Once reached, their soul memory banks will get triggered (if they haven't been already) and they will be the ones who bring in Unity consciousness and Holistic ways of using the Earth's energies, to remove dependence on fossil fuels. They will bring the planet back into balance and harmony. They are specialists too, and I call them the **Volunteer Task Force**.

Others are from soul groups which have been in-volved with Earth for millennia, who came here fleeing from the Wars of the Heavens, especially those who blew up their own planet, Marduk, which was between Mars and Jupiter. They are the ones who control the planet at the present time (I call them the **Infiltrators**).

When you start seeing this bigger picture, you understand your soul is not here by some fluke, but rather by design, and it is not your *Whole* soul, but merely a fraction of it.

In some cases, when a planet is about to ascend, and thus move into a higher frequency band or conscious-ness (as is the case with the entire *Milky Way Galaxy* at the moment) more than one part of the soul will incarnate. I call these souls *Twin Flames*, for want of better words to describe them.

A *Twin Flame* differs from a Soul Mate, in that the Soul Mate comes from the same *Soul Group* e.g. *The Loving Ones*, and a *Twin Flame* comes from the *Same Soul*, thus is one of the 12 flames which make up your soul.

The soul is equally divided into masculine and feminine parts, as is all of Creation. This is balanced, for everything in Creation has a positive and negative charge. In essence, a particle of the soul will have either a greater negative or positive charge, remembering that this is pure light frequency.

Have you ever been in a science class where a positively charged ball meets a negatively charged ball, and electromagnetic energy explodes where they meet? This is essentially what happens if two parts of the same soul meet on this planet – an immense spark ignites, which is expressed as sexual arousal, but unfortunately that is where most people stop.

True relationships are not just about sex, but rather a profound sense of *intimacy*, which goes beyond good sex.

In the depth of Intimacy, lies Trust.

If I can, at a deep and profound soul and heart level, stand naked, vulnerable and open before my Twin flame, totally open, with light and shadow, nothing hidden whatsoever, no secret agendas, nothing but the absolute purity and innocence of my soul, and trust the other to become *at-one* with me, totally open at soul level, and stripped naked to the core, then the two flames merge *As One* and create a Third Force, which is the Sophia or Holy Sacred Flame.

As long as I have closed off parts of me, which are not in higher alignment, balance and harmony, the Flame of my Twin will consume and burn me in all those places where I have not made peace with myself, my counterpart, and most importantly, life itself. All those unloved parts of me, will stand there, waiting for me to own them and love them, before I can do the same in my **mirror relationship**, with my twin flame.

For nobody mirrors you as much as the Twin does, after all they are part and particle of YOU, of your soul. The Twin knows you inside and out, both your shadow and light.

Whatever you hate about yourself, will show up in your Twin. Whatever you love about yourself, will show up in your Twin.

At this time, much of that which has been holding back the true union of these two, is falling apart. Thus if one twin if still in a relationship with another, or not available for some other reason, that too will start disintegrating and falling away.

So many twins have been born at this time, to assist this planet through the greatest upheavals there will be for thousands of years to come. Each pair has their own special assignment and commitment to Higher Service, and thus need to get together now, at this time.

Should one of the pair fail to do so, another soul mate will step in to fill that gap, or they will get invisible help from another one, on the Higher Levels of Consciousness.

This is not a time to shrink. It is a time to step into high gear and know that at this moment in time personal differences (the Twins have plenty), will be put aside for the ultimate quest of unity, and working in tandem.

The Higher Meaning here: The Clarion call is now going out to twins to step up in higher service and ask: "How does this union serve Earth at this time? What did we commit to doing here before we were born?"

My intention in speaking out about this Twin flame hype, is not because I begrudge anyone finding their twin flame (I have and I am being blessed), but to bring it into perspective and balance.

Many may now have the concept that if they are not in a *Twin Flame* relationship, or when their relationships flounder or are mediocre, for example, that there is something wrong with them, or that they are losing out.

The Twin teaches *self-mastery*. To the extent we are the Master and High Priest, or the Mistress and the High Priestess of our own Temple, we are able to bring about a profound union or reunion with our Twin flame.

The union between *Twin Flames*, can be the utmost in ecstasy, bliss and euphoria, or can open up the floodgates of Hades and the Underworld. In essence, that is where we are tested the most. That is where our true initiation into sexual sacred rites happen. It is the opening up of the seven veils of our inner sanctuaries within our own physical bodies and that of our heart, our third eyes and soul.

For to the degree that all these seven layers of be-ing, move into the higher octave of being, which is the

13th elevated state of the Tree of Life itself, the kundalini or serpent energy which we raise in our union, will either burn and consume us, or lift us into the higher dimensions of Being.

Why? There is the secret and hidden chamber between our pituitary and pineal glands which is activated by the serpent energy. If we burn each other rather than unite into one single flame, we short-circuit the energy fields which boomerangs back at us and we are consumed with pain. When we learn to become as one, both flames equally charged, then this chamber ignites and we move in the *sacred and higher realms which are cosmic in proportion, and hold in essence the true knowledge of the Tree of Life – the knowledge of eternal life.*

It comes back to the soul empowerment of both partners, before the ultimate in union can happen. All roads in life, lead within.

Until I nurture the sacredness and sanctity of my whole being, and become **At-one** within, I cannot ignite the same in my Twin flame and become At-one with them.

The cosmic dance of the Twins, is in reality the cosmic dance of the masculine and feminine and the flame of **Atoness** – harmony, balance and bliss.

I AM the Goddess

Of a thousand stars
Galaxies sprinkling
Out of my fingertips…
Luscious curves

Of my body
Eternal allure
The Mystery…
Eternal Mystery
WOMAN
Yes
WOMAN
Am I….
When I see myself
Reflected
In the dark pools
Of your eyes,
When I feel the
Red-hot
Awakening
Of your powerful
sword…
When the
Man
And wo-man
Dissolve
Into
One
Then the
Waves
Upon
Waves

Of
Concentric
Flames
Enter
The
Halls
Of
Bliss
Ecstasy
Euphoria
Delight
I AM completed
In
You.
Eternally
Mystically
One.
God and Goddess…
Sun and Moon…
Mystical
Alchemical
Sacred
AS ONE…..

Judith Küsel

Chapter 21

The Illuminated Twin Flames and Reunion in 2012 – 2017

In the beginning, when the first souls and soul groups were birthed, many of these new souls decided to assume an *androgynous* form, with male and female in the same body.

A soul consists of pure energy, and within a soul, there are a million shards or pieces of soul in the form of particles of energy, which are the male and female, or positively and negatively charged particles. They form what appears as a spiralling form of energy, which, at its most extended part, makes a concentric circle. This is the **androgynous** form.

At one stage in the evolution of intelligent life, and thus the evolution of a human-like form, many souls wanted to experience life in the more distinct male and female aspects of form. Thus a certain number of souls, volunteered to take on a solely male form to experience the more masculine side of life and their other halves the more feminine side of life.

The Divine Source has two definite parts, the male and female aspects, and both are different forms of the same entity or life expression. Creation was birthed in the first act of the coming together of these two polarities, and from this seed planted within the womb of the Divine Mother, all other life forms were created.

The *Androgynous form* was mainly taken on by those who serve the Divine Source in some way, the Archangels, Angels, Elohim, Cherubim etc. They have no other form, and in this androgynous form they express both polarities, yet sometimes lean more towards one form than the other, such as Archangel Michael, the masculine form, or the more feminine polarity expressed by Archangel Gabriel.

The other life-forms, including humans and those from myriads of galaxies and star systems, decided to take on a distinct masculine or feminine form. All were created in the likeness of the Divine Source, thus the Father God and Mother God. Yet we are describing extremely potent and high energies, expressing themselves in a form we would recognize as a male and female body type.

At this time the first *androgynous souls* decided they would also like to become distinctively male and female, so their souls were split in half and the soul which had been in one body, now inhabited two bodies or forms. Most of these stemmed from the Angelic and Archangelic Realms and those who vibrated at that frequency.

This is something that few people realize. Within your soul group, you might not *have* these previously androgynous souls, since they had immediately taken on the form of either masculine or feminine expressions

200

of the Divine (for instance, in the younger soul groups)

Those of the Archangelic and Angelic forms who took on a human-like form, were called the "*Shining or Illuminated Ones*", and they formed a hierarchy which was distinct in the vast cosmic scale. These souls emit a very high frequency light and thus, when these two merge in sexual union, (and sacred sexual rites are performed) they emit intensely, powerful rays.

These souls form a cluster within one distinctive group of souls, which consists of *144, 000* souls only. Not more! This was the number that the Divine Source allowed to take on human, or human-like forms.

The other soul groups consist of Soul Mates, and are comparable to the *Twin Flames,* but only at a certain level. Although very much alike and compatible, enhancing each other, they can never reach as potent an energy in their union, simply because the vibrational frequency of their souls, is not of the same make-up as the soul group that the *Illuminated Twin Flames* belong to.

Now, I know that this is confusing. It is not to say that a Soul Mate cannot be a *Twin Flame* and experience a beautiful and high vibrational union, simply that it hasn't the potency as *Twin Flames* from the Illuminated Soul Group have, mainly because they first saw life in the Angelic Realms.

I will be elaborating on the *Twin Flames* of the Illuminated Soul Group, as they have been involved with this planet from the very beginning, and have returned now, to dance the dance of love and life here, reunite and assist this planet with their union.

The Illuminated Soul Group, mainly originate from *Andromeda, Pegasus, Arcturus, and the Pleaides.* This is where the first soul *Cluster Group* of the Illuminated Ones started to work.

Earth was first colonized from these galaxies, and the first continent (remembering there was only one continent at that time) by scientists from these galaxies.

When this continent first encountered trouble with the Web of Light, (after an asteroid hit the planet and threw the whole grid out of balance), the Intergalactic Council asked for *Twin Flames* from the Illuminated Soul Group to volunteer to assist with the whole process of healing the Web.

Thus the first ones from Andromeda and Pegasus arrived and in a specific ritual performed through sexual union, the grid was repaired. (I will not touch on other aspects here, just this). There are many factors involved here, not only the fact that the twins emit such high frequency light, but the ritual had to be done within a certain environment with the aid of particular structures and tools.

During the course of the history of this planet, more and more *Twin Flames* incarnated here. However, during the great fall into oblivion that we experienced on numerous occasions (Elysium, Lemuria, Atlantis, etc.) they were somehow separated, and so accumulated a heap of karma. They began to assume distinctive male and female forms in their incarnations, and repeated the same patterns time and again.

In this process the twins became separated from

their other half and so felt incomplete at some deep soul level.

Right now, a few hundred of these Illuminated *Twin Flames* have incarnated, with their loads of karma. Their life challenge is to find each other again, and to work towards balance and equilibrium, so that their energies may reunite again, and then to eventually use these in the ancient form of sacred sexual union, so to heal Earth and the Web of Light.

However, and here is the big challenge, these two will literally push each other's buttons, as much as the sexual energies and the magnetism between them will pull them together, they will also spark off each other in their search to find a balance between the male and female aspects or energies within themselves.

What normally strikes people about such *Twin Flames*, is how much alike they are. They might look alike and act in ways that mirror each other, their lives seem to be parallel at some level e.g. both teachers and writers etc.

Yet, on the other side of the coin, they are total opposites and it will show. One will love the limelight and the other shun it. One will love money and the other not really be bothered. One with love travelling, and the other will like to have a nice home base.

When the opposites appear it is here that these two are most challenged to find the ultimate union. The sexual energy between them is so potent, it seems like a vast flame of tremendous energy yet, this has to be tempered by unconditional love and acceptance, and giving each other the freedom to be.

This union is striving for completeness. The perfection of an individual man and woman and the merging of two into one – only then can balance be found.

So the key here is *balance*. When one is more than the other, the scales tip too much to one side and not the other. So they will have a tug-of-war until they reach an equilibrium once more.

Once there is a union and the flame becomes almost consuming, then they will move away from each other again, to give each other space. Then the magnetism will pull them back to center point once again, with the same totally and utterly passionate flame.

These two can never be apart, even if one is on the other side of the world, their souls are so intertwined, they are constantly aware of each other, and their attraction is such that they will always come together, almost in spite of themselves. So woe to anyone who tries to intervene between these two, for they will get burnt!

It is not that they consciously seek this. Often they irritate each other so much that they need space to cool down, or simply to find peace within themselves, where they realize their love for the other is simply unconditional, no matter how much their buttons are pushed!

When both allow their hearts to open up to love, to feel the vulnerability (for somehow your twin knows you better than you know yourself, after all they are your other half), and to let love flow, then they will always find each other again and the Halls of Ecstasy,

Bliss and Euphoria open up for them.

In the approaching years, twins will be called to come together – whether they wish it or not, as they have committed their soul reunion to assist in the healing of the Web of Light. They cannot run away from this commitment, and they will simply find that all obstacles to them being together will be removed, and they will be reunited to work as one.

Those who have already found their twin will find that the potency of their union is increasing, as this planet experiences the shift in consciousness so all Twin Flames will work together, albeit unconsciously at times, to heal Earth through their unions.

Let me not speak of Love

Like platitudes,
Those empty sound-like words,
So much of what is said of Love
Is put out there
Without the soul's deepest longing
Expressed
To the very depth
Of BEING
And ideal Grace
That Knowing
Which goes beyond mere words…..
Let me not speak of Love –
Without my heart

My Soul
Engaging.......
Love held within
The deepest
Sanctuary
The sacred Temple
Of my soul.....
Where utmost purity of intent
Reigns
And abides
And is the core of me....
Let me speak with LOVE,
GRACE, GRATITUDE
Of moments when I glimpsed
The glory, sanctity,
The Blessings
Of sheer ecstasy
Expanded consciousness
Of LOVE
Infused
With BEING
AT-ONE
With All-That-Is-
I lay my utmost purity
The flawless exquisite beauty
Of my Soul
At the very feet of LOVE: –

May Love be my every word

My Being

May Love be what I truly AM

And may the Blessings

Of this Love

Touch the core heart

Soul

Being

Which is yours…..

And may the

Rain of Blessings

Pour forth upon

And into you!

I love

For I can be,

Do,

Am,

Become

No Other

Than the

Love

I Am.

Love Loves!

Judith Küsel

Chapter 22

The Creation of Twin Flames

When *Twin Flames* were created, the Divine wished to make equal parts of that essence of which all Creation exists, and which itself existed of in two distinctive forms within the Greater Whole of the Godhood.

Therefore the Divine created from the energy's substance from a soul, two forms, male and female, so that they would enhance each other. Simultaneously each one would have a part of the other within their being, so that they could understand each other better and find a greater degree of equilibrium, when they truly became as one again.

It was then that creation celebrated the conception and birth of the first *Twin Flames* of the Central Fire of the Central Suns, and they were named Man and Woman. They could only experience the entirety of their true soul, when united as one. So men were created to fit perfectly into wom(b)anhood and in the process of their union, they could create another being by becoming as one.

In the ancient Mystery schools of Egypt and in even earlier times, it was understood that *Twin Flames* had a specific soul purpose and mission to fulfill so acolytes were very carefully screened to ascertain if they met stringent requirements. For the *High Priest and Priestess of the Higher Temples of Ra*, read the soul records of babies when born and drew up astrological charts which confirmed their readings and so such *Twin Flames* from the Great Central Suns were immediately identified, as they had a very specific combination of attributes.

Some were reborn at particular times with certain identification marks which could be interpreted. Many of these symbols and signs were in the etheric bodies, or the higher soul bodies, and those priestesses trained to read them would immediately tell those who were called for higher service.

At the age of three they were then handed over the temple guardians for intensive initiation and training into the secret orders of the Mystery Schools, according to their soul purpose, calling and the higher soul work they had come in to do.

In Ancient times these twins would assume leadership roles in maturity, and would have been trained extensively in the Mysteries and in the ancient sacred sexual rites, which, when old enough, they could partake in.

Such unions were considered sacred, and the sanctity was much honored. It was known that no third party could enter such unions for it would disrupt the sacred creative energy and its focus of uplifting energies with the resulting expanded power, or alchemical marriage. The rites of alchemy and sacred fusion merged and this brought with it a greater cosmic understanding of the higher sun and moon equations, which included the sacred mystical paths.

Often in such unions, the triad would come into play where a twin would take on the neutral role of holding the space, or energy for both, for it was known that such potent energy created between them, was like a double-edged sword and needed to be correctly channeled.

The trinity of **Isis, Osiris** and **Horus**, holds within its core this knowledge.

However simultaneously the twins would create another triad, which was the fusion of the Divine Sun and the Sacred Fire which in turn brought the two triads together, that of the earth and the cosmic Sun. So then the magical powers of the energies were un-leashed, elevating the energies from which you could now literally change yourself and anything else you aspired to. This energy was infused into the life of the mission work these two twins then did. Together.

The Mystical Sacred Union of the Twin Flames was never just for the mundane union some now conceive it to be, but rather as a specific mystical pathway towards the full radiation of the Central Sun with the two, and then in alchemical fusion to amplify this energy bringing massive consciousness changes in all whose lives it touched.

It was that central leadership role, that full Christedness which emerged once the higher initiatory status was reached when you could then channel this energy completely into the work amplified by these energies. These souls in total higher service would create this energy between them, which would uplift and enhance the rest of the lives of those they ruled over.

It was a highly spiritual soul path, a Mystic path, different from any other. It was higher path of love, which truly became an alchemical force. You never embarked on such a pathway lightly but with total dedication knowing intrinsically that this was never about the ego, but about combined work of higher service agreed to render and complete in this incarnation.

These are the higher pathways of the Mysteries, often called the Higher Pathways of Destiny and Fate, as you would literally become the path, in order to be transformed into that higher Sun Path, of the Great Central Sun.

The initiations along the Sun Path, were incredibly severe and few ever made it to the top, mainly because if you couldn't hold the alchemical fusion and sacred fire energies if your vibrational frequency had sunk too low, you would disintegrate at some level. It was only the strongest who ever made it and were empowered with inner strength, with inner Illumination, and with that Mystical Energy. You embraced the higher paths of resurrection, then ascension, in an illuminated mystical way.

You had to die to the old earth self, and assume that which was not of the earth but totally of the **Illumined Central Sun**. You retained your physical form yes, to do the work here, but were in a different vibrational cosmic state.

In such alchemical unions commitment and the total understanding and agreement to walk this path together formed an essential ingredient. If not willing to totally disintegrate upon yourself to be revamped, reinvented, and stretched beyond the norm, then such a path was not open, but blocked on many levels. For those *Twin Flames* who inherently know this, and have now returned, these Sun Paths are something they remember deep down, and when meeting their twin, immediately recognize and know this.

Many have had to endure stringent initiations in the inner planes in the last few years, and often felt all was disintegrating and dissolved. Those initiations were meant to prepare these souls for the highest possible mission, and they know this. Most have an immense sense of higher calling and purpose and are driven. To them this is the only path, the highest possible path and so when coming together they have total dedication to this path and service and to each other and the Divine, demanding all.

We have to start acknowledging the shadow, the dark within ourselves, to the same degree as we have and often do acknowledge the light or good side.

We are not alone in this process. We are given tools and the assistance we need. All we have to do, is ask. Great Cosmic Masters, Beings, Angels and Archangels are there to aid us. The Unicorns are here in great numbers too, and will always assist individuals whose highest aspirations are to serve the Higher Good.

To really work with these cosmic energies, it is important to first go within. All the tools, the knowledge that we need, is there, right within us and our connection to our soul group or Over-Soul and the Divine Source. Many of our soul mates have incarnated at this time and we will meet up with many more in the near future. We will start working as a complete unit, those who are incarnated with those assisting from the Higher Realms.

Twin Flames will be reunited even if they seem to have parted or simply found the challenge of *Twin Flame* relationship too hot to handle, for it is a question of bringing two opposing energy fields into perfect harmony and equilibrium. The two cannot merge for too long a period, before the one will move to the outer circle while one remains in the inner circle. Then both will move out to the end of the circle before being drawn together again. This awakens emotions and passion not experienced in any other relationship. The aim here is to find the state of equilibrium within this relationship, despite the challenges.

Twin Flames will find that equilibrium within the next three years, and then those who volunteered will remember all and act upon the opening of energy centres, which only they can do, through their union. When merged in sexual union, tremendous energy forces are released, and when done in a certain milieu (which is too potent for me to reveal here) they can literally light up the world's energy centres and reconnect these to the Ancient Cosmic Ones.

Here Ancient Sexual Rites are involved, which

even the most secret societies and those who follow the Isis cults, do not know about. These rites were removed from this planet, because of their potency efficacy, and so are not be misused for the wrong purposes (as some tend to do).

Every single soul is now going to find that they will start searching more and more for the truth as it reveals itself.

Truth, pure and true is never comfortable.

There are but a handful of such twins incarnated and they know who they are.

They have always done this work in other incarnations, in other dimensions, and life forms for they are cosmic and not of this earth.

Let those who have ears – listen with the inner ear.

Let those who have eyes – see with the inner eyes.

Let those who know – embark.

The time is NOW!

There are a thousand ways to say: I LOVE YOU!

A myriad ways to show….

Heart will seek heart…

Soul seek soul…

Through time and space and all Eternity…

Love is an irresistible magnet…

always drawing to it…

what truly belongs to you….

Love is always just a breath away…

and when you truly love…
the other is as much a part of you…
as your own breath…
heartbeat…
and the life-giving force
that's you!
There are a thousand ways to express
the LOVE that's you!

Judith Küsel

Chapter 23

Twin Flames, Sacred Union and Sexual Energies

When the Divine Source was birthed, when that very first union between the *Divine Masculine and Feminine* occurred, it was the first sacred union between the two energies and with it came the first orgasm and then, the first seed was sown in the Divine Feminine from which all of Creation came forth.

Out of Divine Sacred Union, when the male and female aspects of the Divine Godhead became as one flame, Life was conceived and from this, new forms of life were created.

Within one single incarnation, there is still only a tiny fraction of a particle incarnated on Earth as one quarter always remains with the Divine Source, and one quarter attached to the Galaxy of origin. On earth now, there would be only a part of the whole soul incarnated. This is vital to understanding of the *Twin Flames* relationships and one which few people have a concept of an understanding.

In order for the soul to experience life in its myriad forms, it reflects aspects of life, emotions and experiences back to the Divine Source from where it comes. Sexual energy in its highest form will always reflect that first moment of bliss, ecstasy and sheer extended beingness of the first Divine union as it does all other aspects of life.

Within one Soul Group there are 144 souls, and within each of these there are *Soul Clusters*, comprising of 12 souls uniting within a circle, which then form the 13th life-creating form. This is another vital component of *Twin Flame* love which we have forgotten about.

In times of great change or upheaval at a certain point in Creation, particular Soul Groups will take it upon themselves, to incarnate onto a planet or galaxy, in order to co-create. By combining the flames of the twin souls within one cluster, this raises the frequency and vibration of that system. The whole Cluster *will have within their soul contracts, the agreement to unite to bring about the Ascension of their Soul Groups and* Clusters. *These will be brought into a higher dimension or state of being.*

At this moment, this is exactly what is happening. Certain Soul Groups have taken it upon themselves to raise the frequency and vibration of earth, to lift it up into a *higher state of consciousness by uniting their flames* and then as a *Collective group to ascend into higher states of consciousness* which is an evolutionary state. Thus, Soul Groups will be evolving into even higher and higher dimensions and states of Being.

I need to get this message across so that an understanding can dawn that you may have more than one single *Twin Flame* within Clusters of a Soul Group, which would then be a Single Entity or further, a division into 12 equal parts, male and female.

*The whole Twin Flames relationship is about frequencies, vibrations and the soul vibrations or flames merging into **one single flame**. Thus it is essentially about creating balance, the perfect balance between two complete parts.*

It is never about the one fulfilling the other, or filling the unfilled parts, but of each single entity being complete in itself, balanced and then merging with the balanced whole of the other.

If there is any disparity whatsoever, then this relationship will be one of the most challenging there is, for if one is too much, and the other too little, then the flame created will devour and scorch and there will be multiplied pain and frustration in this relationship, more so than any other, for love has to be balanced and therefore unconditional.

Within *Twin Flames* relationships, the sexual energies released are immensely powerful and more profound than in any other kind of relationship. Here we will have to relearn the true meaning of how to use sexual energies correctly. For any misuse will always lead to self-servicing, self-gratification, control, abuse and the misuse of orgasms which in the end will be destructive instead of creative.

Twin Flames love is essentially about the higher chakras so that the activation and full use of the 12 chakra energy systems can be combined with the full activation of the spinal cord energies in all 33 vertebrae. This would include the base chakra to the heart upwards via the crown chakra, the Soul Star Chakra and up through the Stellar Gateway connecting to the Divine Union and then back to the heart center. If orgasms are released via the base chakra then the sexual energy is completely lost and not used correctly.

We are now talking about the essential life forces or prana energies which have a life-enhancing force and if used in the correct manner will have transcendental effects and will literally push the sexual experience into the realms of blissful higher dimensions.

Yet, if this union is not intended to create immense love and respect for the other, nor acknowledged as essentially Sacred, then this engaging will be a constant pulling of energies to the one or the other. It will then become rather a dividing force and not a united flame.

There are ancient methods of achieving this perfection, and I am not referring to tantric sex, which includes the white and the black. The Ancients understood *Twin Flames* sexuality more than we currently do. They understood the potency of the released energies, and had a full understanding of the Creative Flame and energies created and knew just how to channel this in the correct manner to enhance the life-force. This in turn led to longer life, expanded energy, and a connection to the heart energy center of earth and beyond that to the Cosmic heart.

As I have mentioned previously, I often have people telling me from around the world that they have met their *Twin Flame* but there is no recognition of this fact from the twin. But rather the other is not recognizing this, or had recognized it and then ran away, or is lost somewhere along the line. It is important to remember that this will happen, for again, the notion of balance is essential. If you are in the 5th dimensional state and your twin is still stuck in the 3rd, then you are out of balance, for you are too much and they too little, so the scales will be tipping either the one way or the other. No glue in the all the world is going to make that balance come about, forcing this to happen will just put more strain on the whole relationship.

One must understand that the soul is eternal. There is not just this lifetime to sort out problems. In other dimensions and states of Being, you well might be in perfect balance and harmony and it is just that life on this planet tends to seduce some to forget who and what they truly are. So, instead of trying desperately to make things work out, know that there might be other twin souls from the cluster of 12, who may fill the gap or become your soul mate; the Divine will always bring you what your soul needs to learn or experience at the right time.

Within the Cluster of souls, when all 12 unite, tremendous energies are collectively released which will push this Cluster into advanced states of being. However, when all 12 unite, they have a specific mission to fulfil. They will do this in higher service to the divine with the full knowledge that they have returned to do this.

Not everybody has a twin who has incarnated at this time. Most often, the twin will act as a higher guide and be there for the other in many ways; the twins will unite in their sleep states.

Some of the souls incarnated at this time are highly evolved beings with extraordinary frequencies and have a difficult time finding anyone on this plane who can match their soul frequencies. Generally, it is not likely that they will find that particular and special one, but if they make peace with this and dedicate their lives to the higher service of the divine, they will find love and sexual energy fulfilment in many other ways, without the added challenge of life here interfering. The highest expression and experience of this potent sexual energy occurs when souls merge with light bodies; this is truly transcendental!

Within the higher meaning and scheme of things, no-one is ever without love or deprived of anything. All is perfect and whole and complete.

With you

It's a home-coming..

A place of Love…

With you

Galaxies, stars and star systems

Expand… simply expand….

With

Words can't express

The ultimate

Beingness…

Bliss…

Euphoric

Rebirthing…

When all you are

I am

Merges as ONE!

Judith Küsel

Chapter 24

The Coming Together

There is a tremendous magnetic pull right now, which draws *Twin Flames*, soul mates and Soul Group families together.

Your own family might have been chosen by you for various reasons, yet you also have a *Soul Family*, which normally means *a core group of souls within a Soul Group who have always worked together on special assignments* and who are currently being pulled together to complete the work that has begun here when earth was first formed and then civilized.

The irresistible attraction is so strong because these souls cannot activate their own true potential until the collective group is in place. By combining their joint powers and knowledge, the Over-Soul's collective higher healing, teachings and knowledge will come to the fore and become the impetus that earth requires to move forward.

I work with souls, mainly because this is what I have always done, lifetime after lifetime, yet I also work with and anchor in vibrational frequencies. This is why I can read landscapes and energy lines which others cannot do. In many ways, I have to be a pioneer until everyone else catches up, which is what we as **Illumined Ones** *are programmed to do.* I know that within my Soul Group there are certain souls, with whom I have united time and again to work for the higher good of humanity.

What happens in such a case is like a beehive and the honeycomb. There are cells within the honeycomb which form one entity. Each cell has its own function which is amplified by all the other cells so it becomes a powerhouse, emitting strong energies.

The same occurs within soul family groups. They will normally occur in clusters of 12 souls and their combined energy becomes the 13th power. This becomes the creative force.

In this, there is great hidden meaning. There were originally 12 Pyramid Temples, 12 Crystal Skulls, 12 Crystal Keys, 12 High Priests and Priestesses from 12 Galaxies, which formed the first civilization here in Africa; this was called Elysium. The combined keys and codes were held within the 12th dimension. The 12th and 13th dimension combined completed the whole and became an alchemical fusion of immense power.

This number is reflected in the 12 tribes and the 12 disciples.

At this moment, there is a clarion call for the 12 making up a soul group who have always worked together to link up once more.

Once this happens, they will contribute a remarkable impetus to the work individuals have been doing for some time. It will unite high ranking, highly evolved master souls who have all the higher knowledge, teachings and healing abilities to truly bring this as a collective gift back to us.

Some Soul Groups are more evolved than others, yet the 12 Soul Group's most active here at this time, work as a unit. They stem from the 12 Master Galaxies and thus they have all the knowledge of the Ages at their fingertips.

Some are here to heal the nature kingdom, some the mineral and elemental kingdoms, some the animal, bird and fish kingdoms and so forth. Each has a different task and not all are equally empowered as each galaxy brings in a different viewpoint on life and life forms.

The highest ranking ones here at this time are the **Illumined Ones**. They are supremely evolved master souls, and within their own Soul Group there are also different octaves of evolvement. They are here for the collective healing of humanity. They are here to bring light, to reactivate the pyramids and the *Web of Light*. They hold the central codes and keys.

When these groups empower themselves, they begin to radiate and transmit at much higher frequencies which then gives them the ability to lift the rest of us more easily into the higher dimensions.

For this planet is now being pulled further into the wormhole through which this solar system, its sun, and the two universes to which it belongs, together with the Milky Way Galaxy are also being drawn into. With this, the whole will experience a total re-birthing into more evolved states of consciousness.

As more and more of these groups are activated,

energy centers will be opened up with a mass of generated energy accelerating the entire rising of consciousness in an intense way.

Another Soul Group which urgently needed to unite, is the **Graces** for they bring in the grace-filled, higher loving and healing that we all need. They introduce beautiful gifts of forgiveness and release old patterns and this is followed by the amazing sprouting of new love. Many say that they have met their twin and felt the excitement and the energy that is radiated from that meeting. Some want to know why their 'twin' is not with them. It may just be that the other person is married or involved elsewhere. Again, their soul contracts come to into play. If they have had karmic links to other souls in past lives which need to be sorted out, these will take priority. Sometimes, it is a matter of the individual having to master specific lessons before true union can begin. Thus meeting a twin is not going to suddenly have huge upheavals and divorces occurring if that soul does not wish to do so.

For most people fear emerges and there may be a reluctance to let go. The appearance of the 'twin' will not change this, unless of course the other soul decides to sever the relationships and join with the twin.

I know that sometimes there is the hype about the *Twin Flame* relationship being made in heaven but these are probably the most challenging, for balance needs to be found more so than in any other relationship.

We may not choose to hear and feel the essences that whisper nuances and murmurs to our souls. We may grow beyond that, and sometimes it is this that challenges the very essence and beauty of our souls; our innermost wellbeing and the truth of who and what we are.

Then we meet up with those who bring us back to our essential selves and see the inherent shimmering and exquisite beauty of the pearl and rose reflected in our eyes and our being; they remind us of the essence of purity and the perfume of our inmost soul. Each pearl in our hearts forms a string of pearls around the quintessence of our soul.

These are enhanced by the beautiful moments we experience in our lives, moments of exquisite and passionate union with our *Twin Flames*, fractions of moments that become memories that uplift, enliven, soften, inspire and guide us. Those are exuberant times of love, given, received and simply shared from the truth of our hearts. There are many baubles, bangles and beads in life but very few precious and rare, exquisite pearls.

Close your eyes and see, feel and sense your string of pearls. Name the pearls by their name, by place, by experience, by gifts from the spirit, by joy.. ecstasy... bliss...

Then wear them forever as part of you with joy and pride and inner knowing that this is the truth of exquisite beauty and giftedness of your heart and soul. Then, combine them with the essence of rose.

Smile.... feel... touch... sense.... beautiful... beautiful... you!

To Be.... or not to Be?

There are a thousand whispers and nuances

So awake ye, from your sleep and get activated!

Illumined Twin Flame Love

Being reunited with you,
Is like finding
RAREST AND MOST PRECIOUS OF
TREASURES...
Allowing you into the inner sanctuaries of ALL
of me...
I am finding honest Love.....
True Love: –
Not because of force or false fronts....
Not because of what I can get out of it...
Nor you...
With you
The Chalice, the precious chalice
Overflows
From the depths of BEINGNESS
That stems from Halls of the Immortal...
Holding, and cherishing...
Becoming the rarest, unique and most beautiful
vessels ....
Which go beyond the expression
Of mere words.....
Trying to form what is felt deep inside of me,
The very depth of me....
Is profoundly felt....

Experienced…

Treasured…

Cherished…

Nurtured…

Loved…..

True love is immortal…

Eternal…

Birthed in Halls of the Illumined Ones

eons ago….

Part and particle of your soul/mine

Of who and what we TRULY are…..

what expresses you and me…

We reflect in our through our merging…

That very first moment

When the Divine Masculine and Divine
Feminine

Merged in total ATONENESS…

Extended BEINGNESS……

The wonder that birthed to life

Illumined Twin Souls….

THE RETURN TO INNOCENCE…

TO WHAT LOVE TRULY IS…

MYRIAD SOUL EXPRESSIONS

VIBRATIONSTHE ETERNAL DANCE OF
THE FLAMES

WHEN UNITED TWO STRANDS

BURN THE FLAME AS ONE…

The Return of BLISS…

Equilibrium…

Balance…

And brings with immense ENERGIES

RELEASED

TO IGNITE

THE WEB OF LIGHT

Open Energy Centres

Brightness of Brightness

Energies of Energies

Vibration or Vibration

The BLINDING WHITE FLAME: –

The ILLUMINED ONES…..

ONENESS ETERNAL

SEEKING EVER THE LIGHT/LOVE

MERGING AS ONE!

Judith Küsel

LOVING

Chapter 25

Trust

Trust is a gift that comes from deep within the heart and soul.

There is perhaps no greater trust than that of an open and loving heart, wishing to embrace the other totally and utterly, and trusting your partner will honor your sacred space within.

For within each of us there are sacred sanctuaries, the innermost gardens of our hearts. It is here that we cultivate our deepest wishes, dreams, and highest aspirations. It is here that we can sit quietly and think things through. It is here that our inner seeing, hearing, knowing, and instinctual feelings have space to guide us forever onto the pathways of the heart and soul.

It is where we tend the rose gardens of the heart. It is here that we lovingly nurture ourselves, and often retire to when we have been hurt, or are bewildered at a turn of events. It is here that we find our inner strength and resilience – our deepest joy, our most profound feelings and experiences. It is here that we remember bliss.

When we invite another into these most sacred

spaces, and most importantly those inner sanctuaries which are situated within our *sacral chakra*, we need to feel secure, validated and loved. We need to know that we can share our deepest joys, and fears, our most longed-for dreams with the other, and not get ridiculed or laughed at.

We wish the other to embrace us in totality, as we likewise embrace them completely.

When the outside world tries to come in with its incessant chatter and discordant sounds and feelings, it is wise to retreat there for a while, to return back into the heart and soul – to reconnect with what truly matters most, knowing that it is okay to love deeply, utterly, completely, and to allow others in.

Some may not understand the depth and breadth of our love as we do. Others might want to come between us, and sow disharmony, but here, in our private sanctuaries, we allow nobody else in, for this is only between you and me.

And as I open up to receive **All** of you into my most innermost Being, I want you to know, that you are welcome here, a long-awaited soul whom I have loved for all Eternity. I want you to know that I open myself fully; that I want you and I to become as one – *one Heart, one Breath, and one Being.*

Perhaps the greatest love comes when I have seen the depth of your shadow and mine, when we both have been to the underworld of Hades, and emerged into a new spring, a new life and beginning. Then we have come to the state, where love is all there is – truly, completely, and beyond any restriction.

It does not matter anymore what yesterday brought – or what tomorrow may bring.

Here, in this moment there is just Love!

Love in all its expression, nuances, the *life force* itself.

No end and no beginning....

All is One...

One LOVE

One Heart

One Soul....

Let the rest take care of itself.....

We have loved.

The Gods have blessed us.

It is enough....

Ad infinitum....

Judith Küsel

Chapter 26

Touch

Yearning for the touch...
a thousand flights of butterflies enticing,
as tongue and kisses spread a thousand fiery
blankets ......
and then.... finding the peaks of my breast....
first lightly... then more intensely.... until they
stand lusciously proud....
while all becomes one symphony of
sensations......
the wetness finding its spurting fountains..... in
infinite wells......
and my butterfly fingers and the softness of my
mouth find the incredible beauty
that makes manhood shine and strut out.....
as all become harder and steel-strong length
unfolds, and grows,
marvelling at the act of Creation
that brings forth such shining instruments for
transportation to bliss....
and then the portals open in the midst of the
wells....

…. Aflame …. like a mare on heat….
tasting….growing excitement….
until all is aflame!

Then the intense yearning for the mighty
stallion to unleash his mighty sword….
Excalibur …. the thrice-magical……thrusting
deeply…. deeply ….

and the infinite rhythms of the eternal mating
dance between yin and yang, crescendos into
spurting flames…..

Until everything is dissolved into a trillion
stars…

shooting into infinite space…. and then….
as one moment of breath remains suspended in
space….

all becomes multiple expanded convulsions….
expanding….

Space and time cease to exist……

Transported through the 7th Heaven,

where the Gods and Goddesses of Delight….
Ecstasy….. Bliss……

Reign in Immortal Halls…..

the Gardens delighting in the coming together
of all,

Infinite euphoria, on the crest of the wings of
mighty eagles in flight…..

And rising again… with a will of its own….
and a wild yearning for the ever expansive,
Explodes into more…… beautiful, exquisite

unfolding…. of bliss….

Love letters from my heart and soul
flow etched with indigo sky
with the spurring fluffy whiteness of surf
to you…
As the most exquisite pearls
I gathered from the ocean depths of me…
waft forth with equal Love.
I gather
the thousand petals of my
heart–rose
closer
and
prepare
my inner-most sanctuaries…
with loving precious care..
And the spiral dances
into
Eternity…

Judith Küsel

Chapter 27

I am Love

The deep fountains and wells within my heart and soul are stretched like a taut wire today.... A thousand words seem to get stuck between my fingers, as the feelings and thoughts, simply do not want to line up... into mere symbols of words.

How does one try to express, what is there... so deeply... profoundly felt? One is like the taut string of a violin, waiting eagerly for the Maestro's caressing hands, arms and fingers, to ignite one into blossoming notes... which stretch out ad infinitum... until the Maestro... the instrument.... the music... all become **one and the same....**

I float on the strains of long-forgotten melodies, which haunt me through time and space.... I rise up... Illuminated Being.... as lit up from a vast Sun within.... The rays expanding... expanding from deep within..... and simply radiating out..... I just expend myself, like a candle in Service.... I cannot question any more.... **I simply am....**

I delight in this beautiful Being .... suddenly appearing out of the blue.... and as we explore each other... take delight in the simple arts of knowing.... another well deep inside of me, explodes into blossoming Beingness..... I stand in awe.... I participate in the cosmic rhythms of music, to which I simply surrender myself.... in the arms of Love.... I cease to exist, yet existing still.... the me, seems to lose itself, into explosions and spasm of massive energies of Cosmic Light – exploding into myriad strands, – opening new portals of existence.....

I cease to be.... For now I AM ALL..... I am expanded... Yet, I am not me.... I am all... and all is me.... and my dancing partner and I.... are merely the instruments to make beautiful music together.... but it is not us.... it is every single particle of being, entrusted with exquisite Life!

Music... celestial music.... fills my inner ear.... no longer just the strings of one violin, but many instruments... tuning and playing as one.... yet, each is playing its own melody...blending... harmonizing.... reaching for the stars yet to be born.... for the yearning within each cavern... of every single heart yet to love.... Then voices join in.... a heavenly blend of the celestial symphony, and harmony of the cosmic spheres....

All expands.... crescendos out and within.... All is a myriad expression of sound.... of vibrations.... of frequencies.... of Creation......bursting forth exuberantly... into new states of becoming.... the flux and the flow....

Angels sprinkle stardust... and dream the eternal dreams of the Gods and Goddesses who grace the

Immortal Halls of Bliss... Beings gather around dressed in their finery.... simply joyfully joining in dancing and song... All are celebrating in a celestial fashion.... an amazing array!

I am then shown a great Cosmic Mirror and I see that Love... *true Love... reflects... to truly connect to another... One has to reflect the other..... Two blend into one.....*

For in the greater Cosmic Love... there is no division.... no yin and yang... for the marriage of opposites has now become... a sheer embracing of delight.... of deep nurtured caring.... of Love pouring out from the heart, every fibre of Being, connecting on a Cosmic scale...with tenderness... deeply caring tenderness... blending with childlike wonder and awe... at the discovery of a like-mind Being, with whom to frolic and play.... *Making beautiful music together..* as play become interplay..... Strings become fine-tuned, and the Master Composer and Creator is reflected in the way everything dances and blends into hauntingly beautiful melodies, delighting the cosmic ears.....

Making Love becomes an art of creating something greater than the sum total of self.... It becomes an act of worship, of creating beauty..... For Love is an art unto itself....

The mists of the cosmic framework dissolve before my eyes.... and see the Great Mother smiling..... I realize that she has always known this.... her greatest delight... is to teach her children the higher art of creating love... Illuminating the chambers of the Inner Heart, and then blending to the inner chambers of the

Heart of another.... then.... learning to create different harmonies.....expanding.... making exquisite music of heart together.... **as one.....**

As I embrace her in deep, profound gratitude.... I dissolve....

I am Love.... Love is me.... Love is the other.... Love is all there is...

An ode to Love...

Love is a symphony
Of multi-coloured woven strands
Intertwined
In a thousand octaves, the
Music of the spheres.....
When you play me
I vibrate
At frequencies –
Transcending,
Earthly ones....
You touch my very soul
And I end up
Somewhere
on the limb...
A breath between all
time and space....
And hang suspended there....
Tears flow
For I have reached

A point
Where I just cease to be.....
AT-ONE with you
There is no space
Where you're not me
And I 'm not you
We enter the Halls of Ecstasy
As The Eternal ONE!

Judith Küsel

Chapter 28

The Music of the Heart

Believe in the music of the heart! Love always comes to those who give it, and there is no such thing as loving too much. Where the heart is open, love simply flows where it wills and embraces whoever it wills.

This all links up in a profound way with every single soul we meet and nurture. In understanding the higher aspects of this, we also comprehend the sheer sacredness of all souls. For every soul carries within itself the Divine Spark, and is thus a part of the Divine Flame.

Thus every encounter is sacred and holy in its own way, lest we forget that we all stem from the same sacred and sanctified Divine Flame.

We tend to forget this in everyday life, and it helps to be reminded on a daily basis, that every person, plant, animal or life-form carries the same Divine Spark. Let us tread softly, gently and with great Love wherever we go, never underestimating the power of our soul and those around us, and knowing that we are now entering the Age of Love, where the ultimate balance and reverence for all of Life will be returned.

The heart is a treasure trove which is filled to the brink with beautiful Divine gifts. Whoever dives into it, finds an endless supply, as vast as the great expanse of the Cosmic Ocean.... and even greater than this!

Love is a gift, a teacher of beauty and grace, which will change our lives forever.

Gifts from the heart are always authentic and true. They speak of the purity of intent, which only wants the best for the beloved.

Love never intentionally hurts or harms – for it cannot go against itself....

When Twin Souls meet, and begin attuning to each other, they make beautiful music together, for here the true soul's tonal cords intermingle and mix, dancing to the tune of the eternal flux and flow of All Life.

Lovers-at-heart start expressing a myriad of notes and harmonies, uniquely their own. They become co-creators, both composers and musicians who vibrate to the cosmic melodies they create.

This becomes a great cosmic force for transformation, for here the energies are doubly potent, and when they truly learn to dance the dance of life from the heart and the soul, they expand, moving up evolutionary trails, and inventing new forms of expressing life!

When the heart is lit up from within by the *Flame of Love*, it dances merrily, living lightly on this planet, becoming cantered in all, and refusing to buy into illusions.

The heart in its true purity is fragile, like the finest Venetian glass, yet it doesn't mind showing its fragility, for herein also lies its ultimate strength. It allows itself to be vulnerable, and to express its true beauty.

When the heart feels alive and well, it is able to express its most treasured, hauntingly beautiful harmonies.

For to truly love, one must lose oneself, give oneself up to the music, blend in….. become as one, in order to find the self once more.

It is like the space between notes, the pause in the music, before the melody resumes it magical journey. It is increasingly touching; rising to crescendos that span time and space – the most beautiful music is made from the heart.

Love inspires. Love soars above all and flies like an eagle. It dances the eternal love dance with its mate, flying higher and higher than ever before. Then Love does a free-fall, she closes her wings, and he is right there, catching her with his wings! Then the reverse occurs, and he learns to free-fall while she spreads her wings to catch him. This is called **trust!**

When the heart plays its exquisite melodies, perfectly in tune with another, then it feels as if in one single lifetime, it has known the joy of a thousand years of loving.

As the heart's melodies float and drift between Earth and sky…. thousands start listening…. and hearts beats as one!

Songs of the heart…. as sung best, in perfect tune!

The more you become authentic and true, and the more you dance to your inner melody, the more likely you are to attract a person who is in tune and in step with your own soul music! When you both start dancing you create beautiful new music as one!

You start playing each other, like a master violinist will caress his violin, and his fingers will pluck those strings, as his heart and soul only wishes to create something so exquisite, so beautiful and unique that it becomes the expression of the profound inner music, from deep within the fountains of his own being!

Thus a loving Divine creation springs forth, touching, enchanting, and becoming transcendental and mystical!

We cannot truly love another, without truly loving and cherishing ourselves first of all! We cannot create beautiful music with another without having that beautiful music deep within ourselves!

All creations and expressions of love, must come from very deep within our hearts. These stem from the creative Divine Force, linking our minds, bodies and souls. The more we tap into this Source, the more we vibrate at the same frequency of the unique soul group we belong to. This is expressed as a combination of colour, sound and light frequency.

We will start becoming like a magnet for those soul companions who are contracted to seek us out, when our soul vibrations and frequencies match up – then we can create more magic together!

If I could sing a thousand songs…

If I could sing a thousand songs…
And dance to a thousand tunes…

If I could span the depths of time…
And move the Cosmic Whole…
If I could find the words to say…
What is deeply within my soul…
I would not have enough to voice…
What you, Beloved, mean to me!

Judith Küsel

ANTHOLOGY OF POEMS

Poems

As eventide
Stretches out her sultry fingers
Enticed, I hear the whispers of the night…….
As the first stars
Spread their twinkles
Amidst the velvety of skies,
I drift into veiled worlds
Of wonder,
Where magic carpets
Inter-woven
form the threads
Of delicate delights: –
Perfumed by Euphoria
(With sparkling Aphrodite)
And Venus rises
To tiptoe dance
The pulsing rhythms
the music of the night…..

Judith Küsel

Avalon

The music stems from far away
The strains fill my inner ear
And from long forgotten shores
The old refrains are haunting me....
The swirling mists lament
Of yore
When once we lived as one
And there
Amongst the bitter swells
The tide of time has rung.....
The music of the heart and soul
Is interwoven....
Precious strand,
Of high and low....
The rising to crescendo......
The ebbing to a flow: –
The lute is silent now....
Your hands,
the caressed strings
Long forgotten melodies
That you once sung to me......
The mists are swirling, swirling dear
And through it all you rise
Your face, Beloved's still the same
The contours, etched in time....

My fingers know each intimate line
And the flowing of your hair.....
Entwined, entwined forever we...
Entwined in act of
Swirling, twirling energies...
Alchemical creation
Oh swirling, twirling mists of time.....
I embrace your secret vows: −
For once we were ruling Gods
Who had all splendour there
We created all at will and whim
Intoxicated
Reckless
Wild....
We rode the winds
We spanned the skies
We ruled the myriad lands
We were the twelve
Who crowned it all
And dabbled in delight!!!
From our loins
The twelve tribes were born
The twelve that ruled the lands
And from our ever creative hands
The twelve pyramids of the Sun
Held sway the power of all of Planet Earth....
Twelve crystal skulls we had in hand

And twelve the crystal keys....
Yet thirteen is number
Which unlocks, unfolds
Unswirls......
The Master Keys we held in hand...
For we had the power, see....
Now time has come
For us to rise
To very fore once more....
The Awakening of Avalon
Has happened, happened!!!!
See?
Excalibur will rise again...
And so the mystic lands
And twelve
The Gods and Goddesses
Are here
To claim
Their dues....
The thirteenth....
Rise Avalon!!!!
Arise and shine!!!
Arise and shine!!!
Arise and shine!!!
Arise and shine!!!
Arise and shine!!!
Arise and shine!!!

Arise and shine!!!
Threefold the number here!!!

Judith Küsel

Beloved

I found my way back to you
Though time and space…
My heart
open
my soul soaring
to
Galactic heights…
Love vibrating
through the cosmos
intertwined
as
ONE….
Bliss…
Thank you!

Judith Küsel

Beloved 2

Love letters from my heart and soul
flow etched with indigo sky
with the spurring fluffy whiteness of surf
to you…

As the most exquisite pearls
I gathered from the ocean depths of me…
waft forth with equal Love.
I gather
the thousand petals of my
heart–rose
closer
and
prepare
my inner–most sanctuaries…
with loving precious care..
And the spiral dances
into
Eternity…

Judith Kusel

Butterfly wings brushing
Delighting
Exquisitely tantalizing
Swirling twirling
Bringing delight
Exquisite wonderment
Petal by precious petal
Preciously savoured
Until all
Is one symphony
Of multicolour strands

Building crescendo
Explodes
Trillion stars
Transcendent
Transported
Contracting circles
Bliss and delight

Judith Küsel

Come dance with me..

Come dance with me
I am alive
And twirling
With the breeze…..
I sprinkle thousands
Little stars
In brilliant ecstasies….
Come dance with me –
I love your style
Your laughter fills
The Cosmic Whole
With fountains
Of delight……
Come dance with me
And we will find
That life completes
Itself…..

For twirling
In eternity
Reflects
The cosmic dance......

Judith Küsel

Communications from the heart and soul

She has long since stop trying to please a man
She has long since stopped crying
Because she did not fit in
And she never belonged
In the too narrow confines
Of what earthlings
Expected of her.....
The tears have dried up
She has come out of her exile
Out of all that which was imposed upon her.
She is reclaiming her voice
She is learning to express
The inexpressible
The voice the unvoiced.
She is learning to cleanse and clear all the
trauma
The pain
She moves into the ancestral lineages
She is clearing that up....
As Mother Earth is healing

So is she....

And the whole cosmos is cheering her on.

She is finding the there is a great difference
between

Feeling lonely and lost

And choosing to walk one's path alone,

For in truth she is never alone: −

She is finding that she is in the best heavenly
company

Which are not bound by earthly conventions
and false belief systems

And thrive in unconditional love.

She is learning from them every breathing
moment

To stay in her power, her truth, her integrity,

And not to compromise this in any way,

For she has to stay true to her soul,

Her own Creator, and that which she has been
created to express

And reflect back to the Divine.

She finds other soul brothers and sisters who
have been

Through the grinding mill

The dying off of the old Adam and Eve

And who become soul companions

On the new trails she is blazing for the rest
humanity.

They know no competition

For each soul has its own path to walk
And its own shadows to learn to love and work
with and through…..
And each soul has its own unique calling and
purpose
And that which is expressed back to the
Divine….
All have their own place and their own soul
Expression to live
Under the Great Central Suns.
She learns to keep that heart open
No matter what….
She learns to never ever give up…
Even if she feels weary and weak at times,
She always goes out and she lives her quest
And she inspires others along the way
To follow their own…..
She is learning to love and nurture herself
And to find that love truly is everywhere
And it is never absent
Only changes in form and expression
And the Depth of her Being
Finds wonder and awe
In the Miracles of love
Unfolding in her life in so many ways,
Which she never would have found
If she had not the courage to live

Her soul calling and purpose,
Her highest soul truth
And expression –
No matter if she lost family,
Friends, lovers
Along the way.
She blesses them
For they taught
Her valuable lessons
In self-love
And in stretching herself
Beyond the norm
And finally finding
Herself
DEEP WITHIN.
She is LOVE
In expression, and action
And breathing and talking
Dancing and singing
In all she creates
She.
Walks to the beat of her own inner drum
And to the music deep inside her own soul
And sings new songs
From depths of her heart and her BEING
Heart-songs
Love-songs

Creative-songs
In tune with the Cosmos
Where she truly belongs.

Judith Küsel

Has there ever been a time when I did not love you?

How could I not?
You are the other half of me....
In your eyes I see myself reflected
And in your Being –
I exist.
Yes, there were times
When I hated you
Times
when pain tore through me
(Like an open-heart surgery)
ripping me apart...
How could it be otherwise? –
Heart from my heart?
Soul from my soul?
Now I stand
Stripped naked to the very core
Of me....
The nakedness of soul...
Nothing to hide.
Just me.

Just you.
And eyes meet eyes
Tears meet tears...
Heart meets heart...
Soul meet soul...
LOVE meets LOVE
No end and no beginning
Eternally there
LOVE
Flows where it wills
LOVE
You ARE me.
I AM you.
ONE.
LOVE
Ad infinitum....

Judith Küsel

Love and Sun God

Love comes...
Hearts open up
Love settles...
Hearts open up
Love loves because it can do no other than
love...
But human beings,
never satisfied,

find flaws
where love only finds perfection…
Laments
where there is nothing to lament about…
Close hearts
when hearts should stay open
so that love can be freed
to love even more…
And the angels in heaven
look at all of this –
the human dramas,
the human pain …
the human bewilderment…
"Ahh… these human Beings –
instead of welcoming LOVE
in all its myriad of forms and expression
to just unfold –
create their own dramas,
their own unhappiness
discontentment
pain…
Because they reject LOVE
when it arrives
and try to make it fit into their boxes… their
norms…
Love cannot be boxed…
nor controlled…

nor ordered about…

Love loves where it wills

for it can do and be no other –

than

LOVE..

And so I stand before the Masters…. the
Cosmic Hierarchy…

They show me the Sun, the true Sun, the
Immense Being itself…

"True Daughter-of-the-SUNGOD, look at
what is coming …. Look at what is
unfolding…."

And I look… I see….

I see the Sun moving in, magnetizing this planet
into its orbit once more….

The Solar – the RA-BAH-RA – the Infinite
Sun…

I see human beings being transmuted by the fire
of the SUN–God returned…

And from this alchemical fusion a new race
emerges, in a much higher dimensional form –
the new root race of man….

I am given the name of the Ultimate One….

I dissolve into the Sun and it dissolves into
me…

And the new root race of man is born – as the
old vanishes into the mists of creation,
dissolved, dis-rooted, existing no more…

But see, that new race of man – much taller,

reflecting the solar rays of the SUN...
The SUN gods and goddesses returned....

Judith Küsel

Love is.....

Love is ever spiralling outwards and inwards....
It expands in consciousness....
It simply embraces the Beloved,
AS IS...
Love has no ONE DAY about it:
One day when you are perfect, I will love
you...
One day when you have a perfect bank
balance...
A perfect body.... a perfect mind.... perfect
social skills and standing...
Perfect family settings...... perfect
spirituality......
Perfect job.....
Love knows that to wait for
One day to express
Your love and appreciation for the other,
Might be ONE DAY TOO LATE!!!!!
It does not wait to stand at a grave
And lament about love never expressed!!!!
Love is the trust and freedom
To express the innate Being that

Is YOU
And not stand in other's shadow
But always in your own light....
Not smothering the other's
Innate expansion and growth....
It acknowledges that the other
Has a unique soul calling
And contract
That may differ from one's own
Thus lets the other the freedom
To be who and what he/she is
MEANT TO BE
AND EXPRESS!
Love is the ability to grow
into your own greatness
And allow the Beloved
To do the same.....
Love cannot be bought
Nor put into a cage....
It cannot be demanded
Nor conquered....
It very simply IS!!!!
Love knows that love and appreciation
For the other is something that grows
With time.....
It is not the heady excitement of falling
In love....

For that is illusion…..
It embraces the WHOLE –
The Light and the Shadow,
IMPERFECTION, and everything else….
And it states very simply:
I LOVE YOU NO MATTER WHAT!
I LOVE YOU UNCONDITIONALLY

FOR WHO AND WHAT YOU ARE!
Love is greatest energy source
The very life-breath of all….
Love is BEINGNESS
And BEINGNESS
IS LOVE!!!!

Judith Küsel

My heart is opening…
Petal by petal…
Sheer bursting forth
exuberant love dance
enshrining
the inner sanctuaries
where only your
life-force
may enter…
it is here
bliss
unfolds

in multiple
stirrings
euphoric
moments
I love!
Love…
Love
Exquisite
ONE…….

Judith Küsel

The greatest love I can give you
is to be fully present with you,
in heart, body, mind, spirit and soul
and soul–fully connect with you
as you connect with me.
I honor the sacredness within you.
You honor the sacredness with me.
And we create beautiful music together
and dance the cosmic dance of love
in step
in tune
in harmony
immersed with
Grace and Gratitude
for the blessings
that love brings.

The path to true love
Deep and profound love
Love which eternally
spans all dimensions and forms
Seldom is easy
It is in essence a path
which delves deeply into the Unknown
the Unexplored.
It delves into the depths of pain
and the Depths of ecstasy....
It is both the cleaving open
to the very core
where the pain is felt intensely,
the pain
that we brought upon ourselves
by feeling separated...
not whole...
not complete...
Then the merging
of forces
beyond our understanding
and moving into the sublime
the euphoria
and finally coming to the point
where understanding dawns
and gratitude wells up: –
for whatever has gone before

no of no essence…
what has been done –
or not done
loses its impact….
One stands naked
and stripped to the core
one's deepest soul
and the essence thereof
and finds
that there is only LOVE….
In that moment
gratitude
becomes like a mighty Tsunami…
Love…
Only pure and utter Love…
Innocence…
No-thing else…
But
ALL….
Ad infinitum…
Ad infinitum…
Ad infinitum….

Judith Küsel

To me you are precious jewel of my heart…
The one I cherish and keep close to me
I delight in holding you

In savouring the warmth
The energy
The vibration that is you…
You taught me the meaning of closeness
Of opening up
Of living past my fears
To ride out the storms
Of differences
And viewing the world
From two different planes….
Sometimes your knife cut deeply in me
As you pried opened the walls
That I built around all four corners
Of my heart and my soul…..
I find that my love for you
Is so amazing
That words simply do not express
What lies so deeply there….
All I can say…
Is that I love
You more
And more
Each day…..

Judith Küsel

Epilogue

The Greatest Gift of True Love and Sacred Sexual Union, is something so beautiful, and stupendous. It defies words. It is in truth the most intimate, loving and most sacred of the Holiest of Grails.

Both the Beloved and one who loves, are transformed. Something very deep within them shifts, and expands beyond what humanly is possible.

In truth, True Love is a journey of exploration into the Power of Love in union with the Power of Wisdom, and the All-Being!

It is Alchemized Union – in truth the Sacred Grail and a journey into the ultimate state of Bliss, the entering of the 7th Heaven.

It is deeper than the deepest cosmic ocean and wider than the greatest cosmic seas. It is Fire – the Cosmic Sacred Fire in its deepest sense.

Perhaps, one needs to go through the various stages of disintegration, collapses, and all in between, be shred into thousands of pieces, to finally open oneself up to the very core of one's heart, mind, soul and Being. One stands vulnerable, cleaved open, naked to the depths of one's soul. One dissolves in order to be put back together again in order to be able to experience ever greater levels of love and true union.

One skimmed on the surface before.

Now, one is diving into the depths of the All–Being and All–Love. The Sexual Energy, the Merging, become the Sacred Fire which catapults one into the orgasmic Wonder, the Bliss.

Bliss in the form of Divinity – the All–Being, All–Knowing, All–Embracing.

From this All–Being, gratitude arises. One is over-flowing with gratitude, as this miracle, this wonder, the blessings of such a union. The sanctified mystic wonder of it all, which goes beyond expression, nor words. It is a state of Being!

Yes, there always will be upward acceleration as much as downward plunges into the abyss, but then one is here on planet Earth in this incarnation to bridge heaven and earth: – as much as one needs the experi-ence, the infinite states of utter Bliss, one needs to experience the Underworld of Hades as well. It is in transcending the Underworld that one rises up and is reborn into the Highest States of ecstasy, Bliss and Euphoria. One in fact experiences the Divine, Divinity.

Perhaps one is best schooled to understand gift of Brokenness, being cleaved open, when one rises up and is reborn into the highest state of Bliss! Out of ashes the Phoenix rises and rises to ever greater heights.

More than this, the Love embraces trust and a deep appreciation for the Beloved, for one has gone through the whole gamut of emotions, feelings, brokenness, to emerge in very greater and more profound experiences of sheer Bliss and Beingness.

Ultimately within, understanding dawns that the Power of Love, in union with the Power of Wisdom creates the Ultimate State of Being.

For the Wise know that the Quest for the Ultimate State of Love and Sacred Union, lies through the journey of the Soul. As the souls journey through incarnations, parallel lives, existences cosmically, and ever unite through it all with the Beloved, it finds WHOLENESS within Divinity.

Divinity = The Ultimate State of Being.

Exultation.

Exaltation.

Bliss!

A state of Being – beyond the beyond.

Judith Küsel

References

Chap 7 *Fractal Time by Gregg Braden*

Chap 8 *Antoine de St. Exupery, The Little Prince*

Chap 9 *Antoine de St. Exupery, The Little Prince*